PRAYERS
FOR A NEW DAY

Graham Jeffery

This edition published in 1998 by
KEVIN MAYHEW LTD
Rattlesden
Bury St Edmunds
Suffolk IP30 0SZ

ISBN 1 84003 186 7
Catalogue No 1500187

0 1 2 3 4 5 6 7 8 9

Cover illustration: *Red Rooster* by Pierre Christian,
courtesy of Super Stock Ltd, London.
Reproduced by kind permission.
Cover design by Angela Staley
Edited by Michael Forster
Typesetting by Louise Selfe
Printed and bound in Great Britain

Contents

Foreword

Books of prayers can be very threatening as well as joyous things. Like recipe books for those who are short of food, or books on gardening for those who live in a bedsit. How is one supposed to cope with them? Should one feel religious? Is prayer itself one of those things which we are supposed to do but can never quite get the hang of? Or is it rather something we do naturally, spontaneously, especially at those times we think we are doing nothing 'religious' at all; only working on our own, or meeting the children from school?

Prayer must be the most exposed and vulnerable form of writing. For while poetry evokes the world or the human spirit, prayer has to wrestle with the difficulty of being human. Everyone wishes he or she had done better. We pray as we face the sun or look into the dark. We are all candles blowing in the wind, wondering who lit us and who will put us out, and when and how.

Collections of prayers seen like this are no more than expressions of joy and failure, humble and vulnerable biographies in which the soul is exposed, a cry for help to God who lives in others, a longing to do better, and sorrow at the inability to do so. It exposes one's need as well as gratitude, and cannot really be read unless at least one person says, 'Amen'.

Above all I am conscious of our Lord's reticence to give prayers to his disciples as John the Baptist did. It was John whose preaching captured the imagination of the Jewish people and made the waters of Jordan flow again. He gave baptism to the world where Jesus only washed his disciples' feet. He gave great sermons and no doubt helpful prayers, but Jesus, when pressed, said simply pray in this way, live in this manner, followed by that brief collection of homely phrases learned at his mother's knee. He did not say, 'use these words'. Only to live or direct one's life as well as we could in this way.

We follow the spirit then, not imitate the words. And may John the Baptist, herald of Christianity, pray for us, and Jesus, its content, live in us for ever.

GRAHAM JEFFERY
ST ANDREW'S, EDBURTON

For Sarah

Praying the Gospel

In the beginning . . . 1
John 1:1

Long ago God spoke.
It was always
   the same thing he said:
   'I love you'.
He said it
   as he made the world.
He said it
   as he made each living thing.
God spoke to us
   by his prophets.
He spoke,
   but often we did not listen.
He spoke,
   but often we did not understand.
But in these last times
   God has spoken to us
   more clearly.
He has spoken to us
   in his Son.

Come to me all who labour and are heavy laden. 2
Matthew 11:28

My search for friends,
   son, daughter,
   is always a choice of sinners.
Your emptiness,
   and rough exterior
   is all I ever need.

3   *Mary said, 'I am the Lord's handmaid.*
      Let it be according to your word.'
      Luke 1:38

      'Amen' usually comes at the end
          of our prayers, Lord,
          of our attempts to follow you.
      But here, in Mary's verse,
          it's a beginning:
          not mumbled quietly
          at the end of a distant collect,
          but spoken clearly, for you alone.
      Amen.
      So let it be.
      So may he
          be born.

4   *Mary kept all these things in her heart.*
      Luke 2:52

      Who conceived you, Lord,
          this strange idea
          that you can change the world
          by love?
      Was it of God,
          this idea closely held
          in Mary's heart?
      It seemed impractical,
          a thing hardly
          to be attempted.
      But she held it.
      Joseph nourished it,
          the idea took arms and legs,
          grew up,
          and found in Nazareth
          a home.

Then died
   and seemingly
   was lost for ever
   till it rose again
   in us.

. . . and laid him in a manger   5
because there was no room for them at the inn.
Luke 2:7

Your first pulpit still speaks to me, Lord:
   its plain wood, and the child's cry inside it;
   and even the inadequacies of your first congregation,
   the straw and the bare earth.
All these remind me
   that the awkward circumstances of my own temperament
   are no barrier to your coming:
   the wood and straw of my life
   are all you need to be born.

You will find the child wrapped in swaddling clothes   6
and lying in a manger.
Luke 2:12

I sometimes wonder, Lord,
   how far you travelled
   from this poor stable
   where you were born.
The donkey stayed with you,
   appearing again
   as you rode into Jerusalem.
The wood of the crib

kept you company in the carpenter's shop,
and would be there,
along with the world's neglect,
when you died on the cross.
And so, Lord,
bearing this in mind,
I think I can see
your whole story,
your whole love,
on page one of your life.

7   *The birth of the Messiah happened like this.*
Matthew 1:18

The sign of the crib
is to the Gentiles foolishness.
The nature of this birth
is to all of us
a stumbling block.
But as we are born there
and nourished and blessed
in our own awkwardness.
The wood of this crib and cross
becomes for us also
the power of God.

8   *There were shepherds in the fields*
keeping watch over their flocks by night.
Luke 2:8

It takes one shepherd, Lord,
to recognise another.
We who had come in from the fields,

our lives dirty,
our clothes dishevelled,
but our flock safe;
we saw you in your crib,
your tiny fingers
opening and closing,
ready to clasp that crook and staff
which life and our need
would offer to you.
You would grow up
and watch over other souls
by day and night.
You are our shepherd
as we are yours tonight.
Therefore can we lack nothing.

Jesus was born in Bethlehem in Judaea. 9
Matthew 2:1

Begin at Bethlehem,
begin here.
Throw the dice,
needing six to start,
needing two to start.
Mary and Joseph,
then an innkeeper.
His wife to bring the blankets,
shepherds to bring songs,
wise men to bring gifts.
Begin at Bethlehem, Lord.
Begin here.
Begin in my life,
all over again.

10   *We have seen his star in the east . . .*
          Matthew 2:2

          It seems a funny place to start a gospel, Lord,
             miles away in space,
             far away from Jerusalem,
             light years from Bethlehem.
          With a star,
             squandered and burnt out
             by the time its light reached earth.
          And yet, most of your servants, Lord,
             seem to have been the same:
             burnt out, dead and buried
             by the time their words
             were fully understood.
          Yet, dying and neglected,
             lonely and forgotten,
             they point to you.
          And they, especially,
             prepare your way.

11   *The star . . . went before them.*
          Matthew 2:9

          I have sometimes wondered, Lord,
             how you came to choose your star.
          There are so many of them,
             all seeming the same to me.
          'When you have seen one star
             you have seen the lot.'
          And yet, Lord,
             each star has its own place
             in its own constellation,
             its own galaxy.
          And you know them all by name.
          So does each soul
             have its own place,

completing with its life
all other souls,
however many they may be.
And all I ask is that I,
who have my own place
in so great a galaxy of human souls,
may, by my life,
assist at least one of them.

When they saw the star   12
they rejoiced with exceeding great joy.
Matthew 2:10

I like what you said about your star, Lord.
Whatever part of the sky you're in,
you can always shine;
however small you feel,
however dull,
and however lost among so many others.
Millions upon millions,
and most of them brighter, stronger,
more suitable for this job of leading
you have in mind.
But your star shone, Lord.
It was all he had to do
and all he did.
Though he did not know it,
having no sense of his own significance,
no feeling of his own value.
When his light was burnt out,
his work was done,
far away, in a planet
he himself had never dreamed of,
three strangers arrived
tired and exhausted
and found you to welcome them.

13

13   *There came wise men from the east, to Jerusalem.*
Matthew 2:1

That's what I like about you, Lord,
    you begin as you mean to go on,
    breaking down in your earliest days
    the barriers and the distances
    that separate us from each other,
    that seem to separate us from you.
For distance is not only measured in miles, Lord.
It is our loneliness that separates us from each other,
    making us strangers to the world.
Yet you, Lord,
    reach out your hand to touch us.
You touched the leper, and that distance crumbled;
    you spoke to Mary, and her separation vanished.
So, as a baby to these foreign kings,
    you hold out your hand from the crib,
    beginning as you mean to go on.

14   *There was at that time a man in Jerusalem named
Simeon . . .*
    *He had been told by the Spirit that he would not see
death until he had seen the Lord's Christ.*
Luke 2:25, 26

I met you, Lord,
    when my life was over
    and I had no future
    to lay at your feet;
    only inability,
    and the memory of things
    I could have done better.
But you will understand, Lord,
    being at the beginning

and end of every life.
And I, who approach the end of things,
     look forward now
     to a longer acquaintance with you.

Arise! Take the young child and his mother,   15
and flee to Egypt.
Stay there till I tell you it is safe.
Matthew 2:13

Travelling to Egypt,
     one refugee
     in a world of refugees;
     you will have no settled place, Lord,
     where you can lay your head,
     no one to understand you fully,
     no life of ease.
Yet we, Lord,
     insecure as we are
     in faith or temperament,
     ask you, the journeying one,
     to travel with us.

And he arose and took the young child and his mother   16
and came into the land of Israel.
Matthew 2.21

Its been a long journey, Lord,
     and after all this time
     you are still travelling.
     still trying to find accommodation
     in us.

17   *And he came and dwelt in a city called Nazareth.*
     Matthew 2:23

So many roads, Lord,
   and all of them hard to find.
The one to Bethlehem,
   the one to Egypt,
   the road maintained by Romans
   leading to Nazareth.
All these roads are your road;
   you who walk beside us.

18   *And Jesus went down with them to Nazareth,*
     and was obedient to them.
     Luke 2:51

You seem to have spent all your life
   at the carpenter's bench, Lord,
   in one way or another:
   carving the wood,
   hammering the nails,
   saying to your father:
   'Look, Joseph, it is finished,
   this table, this chair,
   which took me three hours to make.'
And then, Lord, when you left home
   and the carpenter's shop behind,
   you went on carving, went on working,
   until at the end you could say:
   'Look, Father,
   this other thing I made:
   it is finished.
   This life of mine,
   completed again with wood and nails,
   taking me thirty years to make.

And for your sake I leave it,
hoping it may be of use
to those who come after.'

Then he went back with them to Nazareth.   19
Luke 2:51

Most of your life is hidden, Lord,
   as mine is also.
Those deep parts of me
   only love can touch.
Those obscure parts only fed
   by my own parents'
   constant attention.
But though Mary and Joseph were first, Lord,
   in their tending of you,
   we who come later
   also emulate them.
Not for us a short sudden conversion.
Only that long tending
   and slow developing
   of your life in me.

There was a man from God, whose name was John.   20
John 1:6

Strictly, Lord,
   John does not belong in your book.
He is not necessary,
   for he came
   six months before;

in his birth,
in his public life and preaching,
even in his death,
he was not all that far ahead of you.
And yet, we all need signposts,
   arrows pointing,
   lives to prepare your life,
   your coming.

21   *When the Jews sent messengers to ask him who he was,*
    John confessed: 'I am not the Christ.'
    John 1:19, 20

I did not ask to be remembered, Lord.
I did not ask for a place in this book,
   or your life.
Not even to be one of your children,
   one of your disciples.
For I, Lord,
   could not carry on
   your work or life.
I could only point:
   a voice proclaiming,
   a signpost directing.
'No, not me.
No, not my words,
   my life,
   for I am not anything
   or anyone at all.
Simply a voice
   leading to you.'

Then Jesus came from Galilee to Jordan　　　　22
to be baptised by John.
Matthew 3:13

This is where it all began, Lord;
　　an ancient monument
　　kept open
　　by public subscriptions.
'Joshua crossed here.'
It all happened
　　a long time ago.
But you cross Jordan again.
You and your cousin
　　make the waters
　　flow again.
And when you cross over
　　your first act
　　is not to see
　　how you can dominate the land.
Only to know
　　how God can bless it again,
　　and help us keep
　　love's commands,
　　Moses' commands.
Then will our land be
　　a promised land,
　　a land entered
　　for the first time.

23 *A voice from heaven said, 'This is my beloved son,*
in whom I am well pleased.'
Matthew 3:17

Do you remember your ordination, Lord?
I suppose you would,
 for a wet time you had of it,
 with John baptising you,
 and your Father's voice easy to hear.
But now, Lord,
 the voice is not so clear,
 with yourself on Calvary,
 and the voices of the soldiers
 crowding out any others.
Yet now, Lord, especially,
 do you comfort us
 who have grown old in your service,
 duller . . . perhaps.
For the voice we heard then
 so clearly at our first starting out,
 will return to comfort us
 at our departing.

24 *The tempter came to him.*
'If you are the Son of God,
tell these stones to become bread.'
Matthew 4:3

As things are, they are.
The stones remained stones for you, Lord,
 as they do for us.
And, though we long for change,
 the hardness of this world
 does not seem to alter.
The stones are still stones

when you come out of the wilderness,
not bread to eat;
and if you fall on them
no angels will hold you up.
And yet, Lord,
we who face the hardness of this world,
and long for change
when the stones remain hard,
now have this consolation:
as we are, so are you in the world.

Is not this Joseph's son?   25
We know his father and mother.
John 6:42

It's nice to be one of a family, Lord.
Not all of us manage it.
But you did, being fortunate
   in your parents.
But you did not leave it there, Lord:
   calling Peter, James and John your brothers,
   Magdalene your sister,
   and all of us
   your own dear children.
So you, Lord,
   who call all the world your family,
   will, if you have your way,
   lose not one.

26 *Jesus went into the Synagogue on the Sabbath day.*
    It was his turn to read the lesson,
    and the reading was from Isaiah:
        'The Spirit of the Lord is upon me,
        because he has sent me
        to announce good news to the poor,
        to proclaim the prisoners' release,
        and sight to those who are blind;
        to let the broken victims go free,
        to proclaim a year of the Lord's favour.'
    When he had finished reading,
    he rolled up the scroll and began to speak:
        'Today, in your very hearing,
        this verse has come true.'
    Luke 4:16-21

    You did not come to dose us with religion, Lord;
        you came to bring us life.
    In you, love of God and love of neighbour
        came off the tablets,
        long venerated,
        took arms and legs,
        and walked among us.
    Not another commandment,
        but the old ones brought to life,
        lived in you, for the first time.
    No longer any need for 'religion'.

27 *I go to prepare a place . . .*
    that where I am you may be also.
    John 14:2

    I am sorry I missed your first coming, Lord.
    I would like to have been there when the boats
        were pulled up out of Galilee's water

and those far away fishermen found
   they had one more friend,
   a purpose in their lives.
I am sorry I missed the sound of the seagulls
   and the price of fish being discussed.
And through it all a new voice saying
   the cost of our redemption was even higher.
I am sorry I missed your first coming, Lord.
Help me to do better
   with your second.

The first thing Andrew did was to find his brother . . .   28
John 1:41

Lord,
   do you still remember Andrew?
He would understand if you didn't.
He being
   the smaller of the two brothers,
   the one you did not call your 'rock',
   the one who did not go with you
   and see you transfigured.
And yet, Lord, it was he
   who brought the two of you together,
   saying to Peter, 'I have found the Christ',
   bringing him to you,
   giving you your chief disciple;
   as he did later
   with that small boy
   and his inadequate picnic.
Again Andrew would stand back,
   and having introduced a miracle,
   ask no more than that,
   to be your servant,

watch the gifts of others
grow in your hands,
the small become many,
the weak and diffident become plentiful.
And yet, Lord,
if he does that
Andrew is indeed
the chief of all apostles:
the man the world ignores,
as it passes by,
following his directions to you.

29   *Follow me.*
        Matthew 4:19

I wish you had come later, Lord;
then I too could have left my nets
and followed you,
hearing you speak, seeing you live,
sharing my life with you;
denying you,
and making the same mistakes,
only to see you rise again.
But then, Lord, you do come
in the same way,
with the same voice speaking to us,
the same life given to us to share.

30   *From that time Jesus began to preach.*
        Matthew 4:17

In many ways, Lord,
  ˙ the crib was your first pulpit.
And if we are not converted

by that love,
by that simplicity,
perhaps it is better
we are not converted at all.
Later, Lord,
you got into Peter's boat.
This was your pulpit, too,
the only seat of learning
you ever occupied.
But it was enough
for us who heard you speaking.
Crowding down
to the water's edge
where sea becomes dry land,
we found ourselves
not just at the edge
of Lake Gennaseret
but at the threshold
of a new world.

And Jesus walking by the Sea of Galilee   31
saw two brothers casting nets into the sea.
Matthew 4:18

We were mending our nets,
just as Andrew and Peter were fishing.
But that's how it is, Lord.
You can't go out to sea
before you have checked the boat;
replaced the old wood,
varnished it,
repaired the holes
in the nets.
You know that.
You spent thirty years

    preparing your life,
    letting Mary and Joseph prepare you.
Only then,
    when their love of you
    was completed,
    were you able to set out on life
    and come to us,
    as you did
    that first day by Galilee.
Helping us to know
    we were not just brothers
    but God's own children also.

32   *And they left their nets and followed him.*
       Matthew 4:20

    You found us fishermen, Lord,
      and made us love's disciples.
    You found us mending nets,
      and sent us out
      to mend the world.

33   *There was a wedding in Cana of Galilee . . .*
     and they ran out of wine.
       John 2:1

    We carry this treasure, Lord,
      in earthen vessels:
      six plain water-pots of stone,

used only to carrying
   the most ordinary water.
Twelve disciples,
   used only to carrying
   the plainest of friendships,
   the most ordinary of lives.
And ourselves also,
   awkward
   and quite unsuited
   to the difficulties of discipleship.
And yet, Lord,
   it is always us,
   the empty ones,
   the inadequate ones,
   that you bless and use.

When the master of ceremonies tasted the water   34
that had been turned into wine he said:
'You have kept the best wine until now.'
John 2:9,10

I did not ask to be filled with wine, Lord;
   ordinary water will be enough.
Though I long sometimes
   for a more exciting life,
   a more illustrious position,
   a better relationship with my children,
   an easier relationship with myself.
And yet,
   being filled with this plain water, Lord,
   I only ask that you pass
   your hand over it,
   changing its contents,
   with all their inadequacy,
   into your wine.

35   *Martha was distracted with her many duties . . .*
     Luke 10:40

You met me in the kitchen, Lord,
   as I fretted and fussed,
   prepared, put ready,
   washed and darned.
But all of it for you, Lord,
   all of it for your comfort.
And if sometimes I prepared too much,
   and the thing prepared
   obscured my view of you . . .
   well . . . you will forgive me.
You, after all, fret and fuss
   over me.

36   *Jesus said: 'Lazarus, come forth',*
     and he did so, still dressed in his white winding cloth.
     John 11:43, 44

Funny you told this story twice, Lord,
   but then I suppose you wanted us to know
   this resurrection of yours,
   with its empty tomb,
   and the stone rolled away,
   and all hope apparently gone,
   is our resurrection
   as well as yours.
You are not the only one to rise from the dead:
   Lazarus does,
   we all do.
In our hearts also
   you roll back the stone,
   and are alive.

Zacchaeus, being a little man, could not see Jesus for　　　37
the crowd.
So he ran on ahead and climbed a sycamore tree.
Luke 19:3, 4

I don't know whether I am coming or going, Lord,
　　but with you I seem to be both!
Coming to you, just as I am,
　　with all the disadvantages of my position;
　　and going with you,
　　my very weaknesses
　　turned to strength.
For if I am your disciple, Lord,
　　there is hope for all your children.

Be quick and come down.　　　38
I want to dine at your house today.
Luke 19:5

I'm a small man, Lord,
　　in more ways than one;
　　always needing other people's approval
　　to give me meaning,
　　to secure me a place in society.
But when I met you, Lord,
　　your love held me up.
Standing on your shoulders
　　I was small no longer.
No need for sycamores now.

39   *Peter said: 'If it is you, Lord,*
bid me come to you over the water.'
Matthew 14:28

It is easy to get out of the boat, Lord,
    and perhaps I did it too easily,
    setting out to follow you
    all those years ago
    when your voice came clearly to me
    across the water.
But then the waves rose higher
    and I was overwhelmed by events,
    not hearing you,
    not seeing you clearly.
Then, Lord, I cried to you again,
    in desperation, not confidence,
    this second time.
And you, always with me,
    held me up.

40   *Jesus said: 'Come.'*
Matthew 14:29

Starting anything is difficult, Lord:
    getting out of the boat,
    leaving behind the familiar smells,
    the nets in place,
    and all the companions of my former life.
And when I had done so, Lord,
    it did not seem any easier;
    and when it was too late to go back
    I found myself drowning
    between two lives:
    the one I had tried to leave,
    the one I was trying to follow.

And yet, Lord,
   all our life is spent here
   in this land of in-between,
   this difficulty of being
   what I want to be.
And you, who love me in this situation now,
   stretch out your hand.

But when he saw the strength of the waves   41
he began to sink.
Matthew 14:30

We have to look at the world, Lord;
   it would be irresponsible not to:
   the difficulties
   which seem to overwhelm us,
   the waves
   getting higher and higher,
   and underneath us
   the frail circumstances and events
   which cannot support us.
Yet, Lord, even if these things
   do stop us looking at you,
   we still cry to you in desperation;
   and our need is enough.

Lord, save me.   42
Matthew 14:30

For a moment, Lord,
   all went well
   as I started out,
   leaving the security of my family's boat,
   going to you across the water.
But then I lost heart,

the waves rising higher,
and the fishing boat – so longed for –
beyond recall.
Then, Lord, in desperation I cried to you,
    not looking to you now, except in fear.
And you, whom I followed so easily,
    so thoughtlessly before,
    were there to hold me.

43   *Jesus replied, 'I saw you under the fig tree.'*
       John 1:48

You met me by the fig tree, Lord;
    in its shade,
    its branches covering me.
And my own family
    with its branches, too,
    spreading everywhere.
They were all around me.
Lord, you like to see your friends
    thus comforted,
    contained in a family situation.
And it is still, perhaps,
    the normal way we meet you,
    the first place we serve you.
But you climb your own tree, Lord.
No branches there.
No family
    except for one or two
    (and they not sheltered either)
    beneath your cross.
And yet from that loneliness
    you bless us,
    you comfort us.
And from that other tree
    without leaves,

without branches,
your family will spread
till no one is lost.
No one left outside.

You are the Christ.   44
Matthew 16:16

You are the Christ.
I call you that today.
I send you out
    to do my work,
    to speak my words,
    and find my spirit
    working in you.

Then Jesus, full of the power of the Spirit,   45
returned to Galilee.
Luke 4:14

Was there something
    in the air that day?
Was there something
    in the sand?
As you called to us
    over the water.
And we who had been
    ordinary men,
    ordinary fishermen,
found ourselves to be
    ordinary no longer.
But your priests, your prophets
    sent out
    into all the world.

46   *Were not ten cleansed? Where are the nine?*
Only this stranger has come back
to give thanks to God.
Luke 17:17

One out of ten, Lord,
   is not a very good score.
But at least you got more for healing:
   ten out of ten for lepers cleansed,
   ten out of ten for Magdalene accepted,
   ten out of ten for Zacchaeus loved,
   and ten out of ten for loving me.

47   *Jesus took her by the hand and said, 'Get up.'*
And at once the little girl got up and walked.
Mark 5:41

I wish you would do it again, Lord:
   take your Church by the hand,
   take your world by the hand,
   and raise her to new life,
   and say to those who mourn:
   'She is not dead but asleep.'
But since, Lord,
   'Church' and 'world' are big words,
   big matters,
   perhaps you would begin
   by raising me.

And there arose a great storm.   48
Waves burst into the ship.
Mark 4:37

I get so worked up, Lord.
There are storms inside me,
   as well as outside;
   difficulties, unfaced decisions,
   past failures,
   things I should have done,
   but somehow avoided.
All these conspire together
   to make a raging storm
   I cannot quell.
But you, who are with me in my failures,
   understand my difficulties,
   and give me peace.

Jesus took the bread and blessed it,   49
and gave it to the people.
John 6:11

I felt so inadequate, Lord,
   standing there, with my five loaves
   and two small fish.
And yet you said to me:
   'It is enough'.
This character,
   this temperament,
   this situation in life,
   is all you ever need.

50 *Now there was plenty of grass there,*
    so the people sat down.
    John 6:10

    I'm glad you noticed the grass, Lord.
    It seemed the only thing in your favour,
        except for the small boy
        and his inadequate picnic,
        and Peter, James and John,
        and your other friends.
    But you took what you had, Lord,
        and gave thanks for it all;
        so that even the weaknesses of my own life
        seem, after this sign,
        enough to feed a world.

51 *And those who had eaten numbered five thousand . . .*
    Matthew 14:21

    You didn't feed all the five thousand;
        raising your voice,
        hectoring, shouting
        so all could hear you.
    Nor did you shake
        all of them by the hand.
    Only by your example
        did you touch us,
        as you shared one boy's picnic,
        and Andrew's doubts,
        and by your kindness made
        all things possible.

Gather up the fragments that remain   52
that nothing may be lost.
John 6:12

Do you remember me, Lord?
I should be surprised if you did.
I was one of those
    on the edge of the crowd.
I caught your voice,
    coming across the wind
    in fragments.
But though I could not catch
    the words you said,
    I think I caught the meaning.
As the five loaves and two small fish,
    one small boy's inadequate picnic,
    spread outward,
    hand to hand,
    different people talking
    different people handing
    your word to me.
So when they arrived, Lord,
    though I was on the edge of the crowd,
    I felt in the middle,
    next door to you.
Eating those loaves
    sharing your words
    receiving your love.
And yes, I passed the bread and fish on afterwards.
In fact, that small picnic
    has been travelling ever since.

53   *And there was a woman*
      who had suffered a flow of blood for twelve years . . .
      Mark 5:25

      They say time is a great healer, Lord.
      It can settle things in other ways too;
          illnesses, or states of mind,
          or just failures.
      After twelve years
          these things are part of you.
      My illness and I
          have become inseparable.
      But you separated them at once, Lord,
          seeing me for myself,
          behind the illness,
          letting me touch you;
          you yourself touching me.
      And releasing my illness from me
          for ever.

54   *A woman who had suffered from a flow of blood*
      for twelve years said to herself:
      'If I touch even his clothes I shall be cured.'
      Mark 5:25, 28

      We all need protection –
          from the world,
          from other people,
          from things that hurt us, Lord.
      We need to know where our life ends
          and other people's begin.
      Building fences to protect ourselves,
          we say without meaning to:
          'Thus far shall you come, and no further.'
      But you had no fences around your life, Lord,

no signs saying, 'Keep out. No entry.'
Whoever touched the outside of your life,
   even the edge of your cloak,
   was noticed and welcomed.
And we,
   who come with illness or habits of life,
   so ingrained as to be part of us,
   touch the very outside of your cloak,
   and are made well.

The Pharisees brought in a woman detected in the very   55
act of adultery . . .
Making her stand out in the middle they said to him,
'In the law Moses laid down that such women are to be stoned.
What do you say about it?'
Jesus knelt down and wrote with his finger on the ground.
John 7:53

Write in the sand again, Lord.
Do not let the world draw attention
   to our misdeeds.
Draw the attention of the world
   to what we wanted to be,
   not what we are.
And when the crowds are gone
   and we are alone,
   you and ourselves together,
   lift up your hands to bless us.
Sending us out to serve you,
   to the Father's glory.

56   *Whoever is without sin among you . . .*
        John 8:7

You loosened our fingers, Lord.
We who had kept the commands
      and clung to them.
Fingers firmly fastened
      round those truths
      we had learned as children.
And though we had never
      kept them entirely,
      we had tried to honour them,
      and felt it our duty to punish others
      who disobeyed more openly.
You wrote in the sand,
      giving us time to think.
Time by your silence to remember
      what our own fingers had done.
Then one by one
      we dropped our stones,
      loosening our attachment
      to an old punishment.
But clinging afresh
      to those old truths
      you had yourself
      rekindled in us.
That all of us,
      beginning with the oldest,
      used stones best
      for building,
      not for casting down.

There was once a rich man who dressed in purple and   *57*
fine linen, and feasted in great magnificence every day.
At his gate, covered with sores, lay a poor man . . .
Luke 16:19, 20

It is funny how blind I am, Lord,
    and I became so gradually.
This unusual form of blindness
    allows me to see distant objects,
    and people I look forward to meeting,
    while those on my own doorstep
    I hardly notice.
Seeing them every day
    they become so much part
    of my mental landscape
    as to be invisible;
    and the six or seven yards
    which separate them from me every morning
    becomes the longest distance in the world.
But when, Lord, I realise
    it is you sitting there at my gate,
    greeting me, in your poverty of ideas,
    in your lack of social graces,
    I stop.
And as I stretch out one hand to you,
    or spare one thought,
    if only for a second,
    the longest distance in the world
    becomes the shortest.

58   *. . . desired to be fed with the crumbs*
       that fell from the rich man's table.
       Luke 16:21

What a chance I missed, Lord,
    as I walked past you daily,
    on my way
    to important engagements:
    to those who spoke to me
    in megaphones,
    to those who addressed me
    on headed notepaper.
Because you were so kind
    your very availability
    tricked me,
    misled me.
And, yes, it is true:
    I went to meetings,
    I became famous.
But I never had influence
    where it really mattered.
I never dipped even my finger
    into that vast reservoir of time
    you yourself had given me.
And because I missed that opportunity
    of touching your tongue,
    of blessing love,
    I found I had missed the chance
    of being a missionary,
    not just to one poor man
    but to the world.

John in prison heard what Christ was doing,   59
and sent his own disciples to ask:
'Are you he that should come,
or are we still looking for another?'
Matthew 11:2, 3

The only sunlight some people have, Lord,
   is the feeling that at least
   they were right in choosing you.
When even that comfort is taken away,
   as it is from John,
   their darkness seems complete.
But you send your message, Lord:
   the blind see,
   the poor are fed,
   and we also,
   who see no light at all,
   have the good news told to us.

He met two men, possessed with devils,   60
coming out of the tombs.
Matthew 8:28

So many of us live in the tombs.
Even when we are not dead
   but technically alive:
able to be a fear and terror
   to others,
and no sort of blessing to anyone,
   least of all ourselves.
But you come to us, Lord.
You speak to us.
You clothe us
   with your love
   and affection.

So that the world marvels
   to see us clothed
   and in our right mind again.
Alive, it may be,
   for the first time.

61   *Are not two sparrows sold for a farthing?*
      Yet not one of them falls to the ground
      without your Father.
      Matthew 10:29

      Lord, you will have noticed us,
         the two of us together,
         only fetching one farthing,
         the smallest coin in human currency.
      But in your currency, Lord,
         we do rather better.
      You have a special place for us,
         the little coins,
         the little animals,
         the little things,
         the little people.
      And so, Lord,
         knowing you are listening,
         we praise you in the morning.

A man was on his way from Jerusalem to Jericho,   62
and fell among thieves.
Luke 10:30

Some people make a mess of their journey, Lord.
I think I was one of those,
    setting off when I was advised not to,
    finding the journey too much for me,
    and left by its difficulties half dead,
    unable to go on.
But then you came,
    stopping your life to take care of me,
    and putting me on your own beast,
    walking yourself beside me.
That has always been our relationship, Lord.
    It always will be.

A priest happened to be passing, but when he saw him   63
he went by on the other side.
Luke 10:31

I'm sorry, Lord!
I think I missed an opportunity.
For though I saw you there,
    and went back later,
    you had gone.
So I travel on,
    treading the deep rivulets of this 'other side',
    well trodden
    and filled with traffic.
And yet I long sometimes
    to swing my vehicle over,
    move my life to your side of the road
    where the poor lie waiting.

64   *But a certain Samaritan came upon him,*
      and was moved to pity.
      Luke 10:33

      Who owns the Jericho road, Lord?
      Whose responsibility is it, anyway?
      You'd have thought they would have improved it,
          made it more safe for traffic,
          done something about this breakdown
          in law and order.
      But when I saw this donkey stop
          and noticed the concern on one traveller's face
          – looking for bandages,
          pouring out oil and wine,
          giving up the use of his own donkey –
      I realised then whose road it really was,
          and never again asked
          why 'they' did nothing about it.
      For after all, Lord,
          this road is my responsibility now.
      You have given the care of it to me.

65   *A certain man had two sons.*
      The younger came to him and said,
      'Give me my share of the inheritance now'.
      Then he went to a far country and squandered it all in
      riotous living . . .
      When he came to himself he said,
      'I know what I shall do. I will go back and return to
      my father '
      Luke 15:11-13, 18

      As soon as I even thought of you
          this rough path
          became part of the way home;
          and even my failures

and lost opportunities,
    as I came back,
    became part of your kindness to me:
    a sign of your love.

It would have been nice   66
    to come back with something, Lord,
    but I had nothing to show
    for my time away.
All you had given me I'd lost,
    the money gone,
    gifts and opportunities wasted.
All I had as I came back
    was the dull failure of my past,
    and a longing for home.
And yet, more than gifts of frankincense,
    these touch your heart,
    and my empty-handedness is enough.

When he was yet a great way off his father saw him.   67
Luke 15:20

I didn't know God was bald, Lord,
    short of breath,
    forgetting to put on his jacket
    and only wearing braces
    in his hurry to get up the road.
I didn't know he had false teeth,
    and that a bad heart condition
    had made him retire early,
    leaving most of the work to the elder son
    he obviously adored.
And yet, as I see him,

waiting so long,
with an eye fixed on the distant hill
where he'd last seen his other son,
an ear listening all these years
for his other son's footsteps
on the drive outside,
I seem to hear,
not just the puffing and panting
of one old man,
but the love of God himself.

68   *The elder son was out in the fields. When he heard the*
      music and dancing he refused to go in.
      Luke 15:25, 28

I was the one who stayed at home, Lord,
    never strayed far away;
    never, perhaps, risked anything,
    being partly dutiful, partly afraid;
    never knowing what it is like
    to see the old family home
    from a distance, in perspective;
    never seeing your dear figure
    running towards me, arms outstretched,
    as if my return
    were the only thing that mattered in the world;
    that I should be
    sure of your love,
    and ready with you
    to welcome my brother
    when he returns.

Each day has troubles enough of its own.   69
Matthew 6:34

Lord, I ask your blessing
   on this moment only.
Nothing else.
Yesterday is past,
   though I often regret it.
Tomorrow will come,
   and I'm often afraid of it.
But this moment only
   can I influence in any way.
And I need your help
   to do it.

I am come to set fire to the earth.   70
Luke 12:49

I'm surprised at your choice of kindling, Lord.
It is not what I would have chosen
   to set the world on fire,
   and light up our hearts for ever.
But you laid the fire
   with twelve poor fishermen,
   then drenched all its hope with your death.
Yet, Lord, this poor, drenched bonfire
   burst into flame.
And our own hearts,
   poor and inadequate.
   still wait for your kindling.

71 *When he came in sight of the city, he wept over it.*
    Luke 19:41

    This trickle of tears,
        a stain on a Jewish cheek.
    Thank you for your tears, Lord.
    They are, in a way,
        a proof of ownership.
    You own us
        because you love us,
        because you cry for us.

72 *Go into the village opposite. You will find a donkey*
    there, as you enter it. Bring it to me. And if anyone
    says anything to you, answer:
    'The Lord has need of it.'
    Luke 19:30, 31

    I thought, Lord,
        you would have done better
        with someone else;
        older, perhaps,
        more settled,
        more fitted to the job.
    I said: 'I am a child,
        I do not know how to speak,
        I do not know how to carry you.'
    But all these words
        died on my lips
        when I heard your voice.
    And knowing you needed me
        I trotted forward.

Jesus went into the temple . . . and overturned the tables   73
of the money changers and those who sold doves.
Matthew 21:12

You have a funny way
    of going to church, Lord.
I half expected you in cassock and stole,
    intoning old psalms
    and reverent, devout hymns.
But you came to upset
    all my tables, Lord,
    all my settled habits of mind
    and assumptions about you,
    taken for granted over many years:
    these are overturned and put to flight.
And so, Lord,
    you who come to fill my life
    with good things
    and kind blessings,
    are welcomed also
    as an emptier.

Go into the city, and a man will meet you carrying a jar   74
of water.
Mark 14:13

This was the only sign you gave us, Lord:
    a man doing a job normally reserved
    for Magdala or Mary.
But when we saw
    the strong helping the weak,
    this strong man
    carrying your pitcher of water,
    we followed him.
And he led us
    to a room which we prepared:

bread and wine upon the table,
and all that was lacking,
your own presence with us at the feast.

75   *I am among you as a servant.*
Luke 22:27

You had no sense of your own value, Lord,
    only of ours,
    and of yourself only
    as you could serve us,
    bless us,
    help us to realise
    God's own potential in us,
    Christ in us, the hope of blessings
    still to come.

76   *The man to whom I give . . . this bread.*
John 13:26

I am glad I was your first communicant, Lord;
    I who needed your love most,
    being most in need of your soul's
    unique contribution.
As your treasurer, I had seen
    your money bag dwindle in weight
    as the crowds left, and you never cashed in
    their goodwill for you,
    their deep gratitude
    at the time of their need.
They would have done anything then.

But you left things, Lord,
   till it was too late;
   and I was the one to crack –
   handing you over to the world to deal with,
   because I could not understand your world.

But your command to me, Lord,
   still stands.
What I have to do,
   I do quickly:
   not hand you over to the world
   in desperation
   at your own failure to convert it,
   but hand your spirit on,
   triumphant.

He took the bread and gave thanks, and broke it.   77
'This is my body.'
Luke 22:19

All your life is here
   in this plain bread we eat,
   this ordinary meal we share.
There is no need,
   now or ever,
   to change or be changed,
   except with your love.
Here, in this ordinary life,
   is all we ever need.

78   *Their voices and those of the chief priests prevailed . . .*
    Luke 23:23

    The structures of life are important,
        though they do tend to align themselves
        against the individual.
    These meetings I attend:
        the Roman army of occupation
        regulating taxes,
        the meetings of the Sanhedrin
        checking out clergy appointments.
    I understand the importance to society
        of rules, customs and decisions.
    But all these killed you, Lord,
        killed the possibility of love.
    You who live according
        to the scriptures,
        are still put to death
        according to our structures.

79   *'Will you also go away?'*
    John 6:67

    It's funny how the small neglects add up, Lord.
    We who forgot to say thank you
        were healed by you,
        in sight or hearing,
        but went on with our miracles,
        forgetting the one who had made
        our miracle possible.
    We did not betray you, Lord,
        for thirty pieces of silver.
    We were not there
        to feel the weight of Judas' money bag
        grow lighter.

But we had made it lighter, Lord,
    by our forgetting to contribute
    to your soul's needs.
We did not run away
    like Peter and the rest.
But then, we were not there to run away.
We had gone on with our lives,
    leaving you to your death.
Don't blame Judas and Peter, Lord.
Blame me.

. . . and when they reached the place called the skull,   80
they crucified him there . . .
Jesus said, 'Father, forgive them; they do not know what they
are doing.'
Luke 23:33, 34

They call Everest the highest mountain.
And yet I think yours was more difficult to climb.
This slow ascent four foot above
    anyone's contradiction.
Oxygen dying out,
    no footholds left for your life on earth.
And yet you went on climbing,
    went on loving,
    went on refusing
    to curse us, or blame us
    who had left you
    no way down.
They call Everest, Lord, the highest mountain.
But your mountain, so difficult to climb,
    has been managed once.
And in the moment of that achievement
    love is made perfect.

81 *Finally, when the mockery was over, they took off the*
    mantle and dressed him in his own clothes.
    Matthew 27:31

I wonder if the soldiers knew
    what they were doing, Lord.
For in stripping you,
    and tearing off your robe,
    they exposed more
    than a carpenter's back for beating.
They showed to the world
    more than one man's vulnerability.
If only they had known it,
    they tore the curtain in the sanctuary as well,
    showing to the world
    not just your nakedness,
    but God's love.

82 *So they came to a place called Golgotha.*
    Matthew 27:33

I don't think I've anything to be proud of, Lord.
We all betray you,
    one way or another;
    or deny you, or run away.
Peter and Andrew,
    and Thomas with his doubting,
    only did what we do now.
They are our brothers,
    like us, needing forgiveness:
    and receiving your love.

A number of women were present, 83
watching from a distance . . .
Matthew 27:55

This part of your death is all your own.
The crowd drifting away
   as quickly as it had come.
The nine lepers not stopping to say
   thank you for the touch,
   thank you for the use of our limbs,
   our old lives restored in a society
   you had opened to us.
And now, at the end,
   not even one out of ten
   to say goodbye.
Three or four only.
Some from a distance waving,
   saying thank you for the memory.
We shall keep it alive.

Judas returned the thirty silver pieces to the chief priests 84
and elders.
'I have sinned. I have brought an innocent man to his death.'
Matthew 27:3, 4

Those who die by their own hand, Lord,
   have a special place in your love.
You appeal to them
   with special marks of your affection.
And if, as now, they seem to betray you,
   you share that death on another tree,
   and perhaps, their dereliction.
You appear to them first of all, in your resurrection
   that they may find, after the darkness,
   a new morning.

85   *I am come that you may have life.*
       John 10:10

       Where do I fit in, Lord?
       That's what I'd like to know.
       Each piece of the jigsaw has its place,
          fits in with others neatly,
          completes the picture.
       But I who have no place
          know that you need me.
       In your design I am invaluable.
       You pick me up.
       You place me.
       You love me.
       You are my friend.

86   *My God, my God, why have you forsaken me?*
       Matthew 27:46

       You used to be in control of events, Lord,
          but now events control you.
       You are held fast by Roman rope
          and nails and wood.
       You cannot speak
          except in sharp sentences of pain.
       You cannot walk.
       And you, who gave sight to the blind,
          now need to see some purpose
          in your own life,
          your own death.

Jesus cried aloud again and breathed his last.   87
Matthew 27:50

Death, your death, not anyone else's.
Blood and hurt, your blood and hurt.
Still, after thirty-three years
    you have not given offence.
You have not done harm.
And so, because you die thus,
    loving us to the end,
    the end of your flesh and blood
    is not the end of love.
You die, your ministry is broken.
But broken into many bits,
    it finds its place in us.
In this spot, love is completed,
    your life is made perfect.

It is accomplished.   88
John 19:30

At least you didn't curse them, Lord.
Grunts or swear words
    I do not count in this context.
But you seem to have managed
    right to the end
    to have avoided harm.
Harm to others, I mean,
    not to yourself.
And so, from this part of your life
    your story starts.
Not finished but complete,
    it begins again in me.

89 *He bowed his head and gave up his spirit.*
    John 19:30

    Why does your silence
        speak to me so loudly?
    No cursing of your enemies,
        no making of points,
        only your life offered,
        your love offered for my sake,
        for my salvation.

90 *Father, into your hands . . .*
    Luke 23:46

    You don't seem to have changed much, Lord.
    The doors were all closed
        when you first came to see us,
        as they are now.
    The doors of the synagogue sliding shut,
        society itself forcing you out,
        and our own hearts, above all,
        still occupied with other things.
    Yet, Lord, though we leave you outside
        in this place of dereliction,
        your life still speaks to us.
    As at Bethlehem, so now:
        'Behold, I stand at the door and knock.'

Now there stood by the cross of Jesus his mother   91
and her sister, Mary, wife of Cleopas,
and Mary of Magdala.
John 19:25

It is strange how you express yourself, Lord:
   a whole life, expressed in three hours,
   a whole love, expressed in one death,
   thirty-three years crystallised
   in one moment of affection:
'Father, for their sakes . . .'
And if it's not too late to say so, Lord,
   thank you for coming,
   though it seemed at the time
   a strange visit:
   the hay and the crib to welcome you,
   not much else.
And now at the end,
   wood and nails again to bid you goodbye.
Yet we, who can only offer
   the wood and straw of our own life,
   are grateful because we know
   you will use us,
   if you will.

And all his acquaintance . . . stood far off.   92
Luke 23:49

There used to be five thousand of us, Lord,
But now for one reason or another
   we are down to two or three.
Or one only, as we look at you,
   hanging on the cross.
You only, love us, pray for us
   in all our extremities.
You only, love us to the end.

93   *It is finished.*
      John 19:30

It takes a long time to make a life, Lord.
So many ordinary days at Joseph's bench;
   so many nails hammered in,
   pieces of wood shaped to order.
And none of it,
   at the time,
   seeming to influence events,
   seeming to change
   the darkness of a hostile world.
Yet in the end you did,
   leaving us not tables and chairs,
   but your own life, now accomplished.

94   In conclusion,
   I have only this to add:
   something I've been trying to say
   for thirty-three years,
   for thirty-three million years.
But only now,
   in these three awkward hours,
   do I seem to find the opportunity
   of summing it all up.
In one word,
   in one life,
   in one death,
   son, daughter,
   I love you.

95   *They shall look on him whom they pierced.*
      John 19:37

It's a pity you died so young, Lord.
You had, after all, no chance

of influencing human history
and making for yourself
a place in it.
Had you lived longer,
Joseph's carpentry business
and Peter's boats also
would no doubt have been established;
memories to you,
extensions of your life on earth.
But dying as you lived, Lord,
in love and obscurity,
you leave no memorial at all,
except our grateful hearts
and you alive inside them.

And you are witnesses of these things.   96
Luke 24:48

A life cut short
but not a life kept short.
For it continues
through the Spirit's power
in us.

Peace be with you.   97
John 20:21

Now that it's all over
I have one or two questions to ask.
Do you regret it, Lord,
this lonely end
after a lonely beginning?
Do you regret
the sheer pain,

>   now it is over;
>   the utter loneliness,
>   now it is complete?
>   Or do you regard your sufferings
>   a small price, the only price;
>   the only way you could in the end
>   befriend me?

98   *. . . all had come to its appointed end . . .*
        John 19:28

>   Job done. Mission accomplished.
>   And the broken soldier looked down
>   at his mother and closest friend.
>   All that was left of his ministry,
>   of his battles on earth,
>   this battle to be himself,
>   his Father's Son in a cruel world.
>   Yet as he said, 'It is finished',
>   they began to know already
>   the perfecting of love
>   in their hearts.

99   *Joseph of Arimathea, being a disciple secretly,*
        begged Pilate that he might take away the body.
        And Nicodemus came as well,
        who had first come to Jesus by night.
        John 19:38, 39

>   I came by night, Lord.
>   Not everyone is brave enough
>   to commit himself
>   more openly.
>   And then, when it was night again,

64

and the sun was setting
on Friday afternoon,
and on your life,
I came with Joseph
to ask your body of Pilate,
to bury you.
It was too late to do more,
  so I did what I could.
And yet, Lord,
  we who serve you,
  shyly and with diffidence,
  also love you.
And we who vote for you uncertainly
  will yet do better.

May we have the body of Jesus?   100
Mark 15:44

And Pilate asked
  were you dead already,
  not realising in this obscure couple –
  one rich, the other shy,
  both weak,
  according to Rome's power –
  Pilate did not recognise in them
  proof already of your life.
For though your body is dead
  taken down from this tree,
  already you work in us
  new life.

101   *Pilate was surprised that he was already dead.*
        Mark 15:44

        I think this was a small resurrection, Lord,
            a small light, shining in the dark,
            two shy men, asking for your body;
            coming to help you
            at the epilogue of your life when it was too late
            and they wished they had come earlier.
        And all they could do was bury you.
        Yet those who come to you
            in the darkest hour, Lord,
            will find you in the morning.

102   *They made the grave secure;*
        sealed with a stone, and guarded.
        Matthew 27:66

        When all hope is gone, Lord,
            you are born.
        When the darkness is complete,
            you come.
        When things are beyond hope,
            in the territory of utter despair,
            we find you.
        You roll back the stone
            and are there to greet us.

He came to the stone and rolled it away.   103
Matthew 28:2

Roll the stone, Lord.
Roll all the stones away
   and keep them rolling,
   those gravestones,
   however solid they appear,
   that stand between myself and love;
   all those situations that keep love away,
   or make less likely
   this great possibility
   of you yourself joining us
   on the world outside.

Mary of Magdala, Mary the mother of James, and Salome   104
brought sweet spices to anoint him.
Very early on the Sunday morning they came to the tomb.
Mark 16:1

I look for you in the wrong places:
   bringing my flowers to recreate old memories,
   my ointment to rub in old situations,
   old friendships.
And yet, Lord,
   you give me something better
   than an old life repeated:
   you give me a new life of my own.

105   *He is risen from the dead*
       and goes before you into Galilee.
       Matthew 28:7

       You were never so alive
          as when you died.
       Never so much present
          as when you left us.
       Never spoke so clearly,
          so cuttingly to our hearts,
          as when you had
          nothing left to say at all,
          except this one word
          heard so clearly,
          accepted so totally now.
       You loved us to the end.

106   *I go to prepare a place for you.*
       John 14:2

       Your resurrection was little use to you, Lord.
       No new life.
       No rekindling of old friendships:
          no saying,
          'Do you remember Galilee
          and that five thousand;
          how we feasted from a small amount
          in an unfashionable place?'
       No use to you,
          but of great use to us,
          who find our lives
          hospitably cared for, loved and fed;
          who find our own lives beginning again.

The kingdom of heaven is among you.   107
Matthew 3:2

How do you measure a man's life?
   Two parents,
   twelve disciples,
   five thousand fed,
   or one death?
One death leading
   after all your sufferings
   to so many resurrections.

He gave them his greeting.   108
Matthew 28:10

I don't know what you said, Lord,
   the exact words you used.
Perhaps it was only 'Shalom',
   your usual greeting.
But to us, then, standing in the garden,
   broken and utterly alone,
   it was a hand on our shoulder,
   and new breath in our lungs.
'Peace,' you said, and still say:
   'Do not be afraid.'

109   *Go quickly and tell his disciples*
he is risen from the dead.
Matthew 28:7

This has been a tough assignment, Lord,
   and still we have hardly begun,
   conveying your love to people in all generations,
   all circumstances of life,
   on different continents.
Yet, however great the distance
   that separates you from us,
   we are still, as Peter and Magdala.
   your brothers and sisters,
   sent into the world.

110   *The same day two of them were on their way to*
Emmaus . . .
As they walked and discussed with one another,
Jesus himself came and walked with them.
But something stopped them knowing who he was.
Luke 24:13-16

When two people walk
   on any journey,
   when two people travel, Lord,
   a long path together,
   there comes a time,
   not easy to pinpoint,
   when all their onward journeying
   bears fruit.
And they find not two,
   but a third person
   travelling their journey
   with them.

We felt our hearts on fire. 111
Luke 24:32

Where two or three meet in love's name
  there you are, Lord,
  among them.
Not only in the stable,
  but by Galilee too,
  James and John,
  Andrew and Peter.
And then at the close
  Peter and John running,
  the two families together,
  and you yourself are alive to both.

That night they went; fishing and toiled all night, 112
catching nothing.
When daybreak came, Jesus himself stood on the shore,
though they did not know it was him.
'Friends,' he cried, 'have you caught anything?'
Then he said, 'Throw your net the other side of the boat.'
And they did so, bringing in so great a catch
that the net began to break.
John 21:3-6

One gets discouraged, Lord,
  when you've gone on as long as I have,
  doing your best with no result.
I have tried every throw of the net,
  everything I am capable of.
But it is now, Lord,
  after a lifetime's failure,
  that you yourself call to me;
  and at your word
  I let down the net.

113 *Jesus stood on the shore.*
John 21:4

I know it's a new day, Lord,
    but the lessons of the night
    do count for something.
Surely you can see that.
Yet, if you tell me to,
    I will obey.
Silly as it sounds,
    and against all my experience,
    I turn round
    and throw down the net
    from the other side of my life.

114 *Will you also go away?*
John 16:32

The importance of being Jesus.
Getting more and more like yourself
    all the time.
And only when the crowds had left
    and we were no longer distracted
    by the disciples' questioning
    and the Pharisees' arguing . . .
    only then,
    all oratory finished,
    all success stripped away,
    could we see the finished work,
    the importance of being Jesus
    to the very end.

Behold I make all things new.   *115*
Revelation 21:5

The cross was your greatest work, Lord.
All those tables and chairs
   each one made to order,
   each one for some specific purpose,
   for some specific person.
But this thing you make
   is for all of us.
A life expressed in three hours.
A death expressed for all of us.
For all of us made available.

Simon, son of John, do you love me?   *116*
John 21:15

Lord, you know how I feel about you.
I do not need to exaggerate
   or make extravagant claims;
   or to compare myself with others,
   some of whom will do better,
   some, it may be, even worse.
But I say that I love you
   as well as I can.
I say that I am your friend.

117 *Peter was sad when Jesus asked him the third time:*
'Do you love me?'
He replied: 'Lord, you know everything.'
John 21:17

It is not easy repeating oneself, Lord,
 saying: 'I love you, and I will follow you',
 for the second and third,
 for the three hundredth time.
Yet we do it, as well as we can.
As young men or women first, more easily.
Then when we are older
 and tied down to the world and life
 by a thousand little cords,
 we say again the old words,
 'Lord, you know that I am your friend.'
And though we say it with awkwardness,
 with rheumatism in our limbs,
 and tiredness and lost opportunities
 in our hearts,
 still you hear us, and receive us.
And lead us on.

118 *If it is my will that he remain until I come,*
what is that to you?
John 21:22

Your servant John lived so long, Lord,
 they thought he would never die,
 but live to see your return.
And perhaps he did not die, Lord,
 but is still here in your Church,
 silently waiting.
Perhaps your Church is,
 in a way,
 John himself,

still waiting, though older,
a sign to all the world
that you will come again;
that peace and justice
shall at last
triumph on earth.

I will go before you into Galilee.   *119*
Matthew 26:32

You said you would see us in Galilee, Lord,
 not in some rare religious experience
 available only to a few,
 but in our old lives,
 our old familiar places,
 fishing nets often mended,
 and a well-known coast.
Here you would appear to us
 and see us regularly,
 till at last we knew what you had always told us:
 that you are with us always.

Go therefore and teach all nations.   *120*
Matthew 28:19

Are we ready to say it yet?
Not 'I believe in one God',
 which is easily said,
 the words tripping appropriately
 off our lips.
But love asks us to go further.
God's love
 impels us to say,
 'I believe . . .
 in one world.'

121   *As he blessed them he was parted from them.*
Luke 24:51

The last picture we have of you, Lord,
   is perhaps the best,
   perhaps the most typical,
   and we shall always remember it.
It is how you lived,
   it is how you died,
   hands raised up to bless us,
   your thirty years on earth complete
   as you make your last journey
   to dwell in our hearts for ever.
For as you lived,
   healing the sick, blessing the poor,
   so are you taken from us,
   blessing us, as you return to the Father.
You do not say goodbye;
   only: 'I am with you always,
   to the end of time.'

122   *I am with you always.*
Matthew 28:20

Don't let go of us, Lord,
   whatever you do.
It's only your love
   prevents us all
   rolling downhill,
   going downhill
   into that dark chaos of nothingness
   from which your spirit long ago called us,
   and still calls.
Don't let go of us, whatever you do.
Whatever we do
   continue to hold us up.

Go, tell all nations   *123*
Matthew 28:19

Lord, you are always with us.
No weakness of ours can keep you away,
    no besetting sin.
In all seasons, and at all times,
    you are with us, till we meet again
    in your kingdom.

Love one another.   *124*
1 John 4:7

We will only be asked
    what we have done to others;
    not how they have treated us.
We will only be asked
    how we have loved.
We can only love,
    where we are allowed to.
Love cannot be forced,
    only offered.
Love can only
    be received.

125 *And the light shone in the darkness,*
and the darkness did not put it out.
John 1:5

It is strange, Lord,
   the effect of a candle:
   so trivial a thing,
   so small a piece of wax.
And yet I light it,
   and for a little space
   the darkness
   is driven back,
   so that the world itself
   is lighter –
   because of my candle,
   because of one good deed,
   because of one life.

Praying the Eucharist

Our souls wait for you, Lord.
It is you who call us to this day,
   and to each other's company.
We wait for your Spirit, Lord.
   Only then can we think.
We wait for your word in our hearts,
   only then can we listen,
   only then can we proclaim.
Come to us, Lord.
Come to us quickly.
Make yourself known to us
   in the bread's breaking.

126

Come to us, Lord,
   in the power of your Spirit.
We do not know what to say
   until you tell us how to think,
   unless you help us to live,
   unless you assist us.
Come to us, Lord.
Come to us now.
In the power of your Son Jesus,
   we praise your name.

127

128   Where two or three are gathered
      in love's name, for love's purpose,
      to listen, not to speak,
      to wait on the Lord,
      not tell him what to do:
      then God is present, love is present,
      and Jesus of Nazareth rises again
      from the tomb.

129   So many blessed by so obscure a life.
      So many fed by one who hungers for our love.
      So many lifted high
        by one who was himself abased.
      So many comforted
        by one who died in loneliness.
      Dear Lord,
        I do not lift my heart to you,
        but ask you to come down
        to where you are already.

130   We brought nothing into this world, Lord.
      We bring nothing into this house,
        this meeting of your people,
        except our needs and emptiness,
        waiting to be filled.
      We brought nothing into this place.
      Fill us now, Lord, with your Spirit.
      Make us your people once again.

The table is prepared, Lord.   *131*
Your table, your feast,
    your love invites us all.
In the company of saints and angels,
    we, your people, love you.
Share with each other
    the life of your Son Jesus,
    made possible for us by your Spirit.
We proclaim him.
We set forth our own faith in his life.
We give you glory.

One thing we ask of you, Lord: *132*
    to dwell in your house,
    in your people,
    in the life of your Son.
We come before you with praises,
    but also with needs,
    and emptiness waiting to be filled.
We wait on your word, Lord.
It directs us and comforts us,
    it feeds us and nourishes our souls.
We sing to your glory.

You visit the earth, Lord.   *133*
Daily in this sacrament
    your word is made flesh
    and dwells among us.
This people gathered,
    this meal prepared, this life set forth
    and proclaimed once again.
We meet in your Spirit, Lord,
    and await your guiding.

134   Dear Lord, your table is ready.
Our chairs set in order,
    each one of us has our proper place
    in your kingdom.
The bread and wine are prepared,
    sacraments of your great love for us,
    you provide for us daily.
The gospels are open,
    that you may speak to us again,
    and we with you.

135   What has been believed,
    by all peoples in all places at all times.
This we proclaim.
This is our faith.
This is our only life.

What has been believed by one person,
    at one time, in one place.
Jesus on his cross,
    loving us to the end.
This is our faith.
This is our only life.

136   We are your people, Lord.
Your holy community.
It is this only,
    according to your grace,
    that makes possible this sacrament of union.
With your whole Church,
    we give you glory.
The living and the departed praise you,
    in union with your Son.

It is not where we are that defines us, Lord,   *137*
    it is where we shall be.
Not who we are, or what we have done,
    but who is at work within us,
    who loves us,
    who leads us.
We meet in your Son's name, Lord,
    but also in our own.
It is you who call us,
    and give us our meaning.

Where two or three meet in your name, Lord,   *138*
    you are there.
Your whole church is there.
We do not come to you on our own.
Peter and Andrew, pray for us.
Mary and Joseph, sustain your child in us.
Dear Lord, we give you glory.

We believe in you, Lord,   *139*
    but also in ourselves.
Our own calling
    by the sea of Galilee,
    our own hearing
    of your word to us.
We come to you, Lord.
We follow.
Not in our own goodness trusting,
    but in your great love,
    we approach
    this holy table.

140   We believe in you, Lord,
        but also in ourselves.
    We are your community,
        your people, waiting to be fed.
    Your people, waiting to be led
        by your word of loving kindness
        for all of us,
        for each one of us.
    Even so, Lord Jesus, come quickly.

141   Lead us in your way, Lord.
    Your word to us is truth.
    Lead us in your paths.
    Your life is our only guide.
    Help us to follow you, Lord,
        even when we cannot see your footsteps.
    Your word leads us in our lives now.

142   We wait for you to act, Lord,
        never ourselves.
    For you to lead us by your star.
    We will follow your star, Lord,
        not our own wishes.
    Not certain where it leads,
        we travel onward.

143   Our time is in your hand,
        Lord, in this moment we are still.
    Not for you to speak,
        but for you to love.

You love us always,
    care for us, redeem us.
Lift us up, Lord,
    help us to hear the sound of your silences
    and the waves on Galilee's beach.
Your silence is louder, Lord,
    than the world's noise and speaking.
In your silence you come to us,
    and lift us high.

I listen to your word, Lord.   *144*
May your wine and oil
    increase in our hearts.
Wine to make glad our hearts,
    oil to be poured
    in our deepest wounds,
    our most tender neglects.
Lord, come to us quickly.

Your life speaks to us, Lord,   *145*
    louder than words,
    but not louder
    than the word of life
    held in our hearts.
Help us to listen to your word,
    and hold it safe.
Help us to see with our eyes,
    to hear with our ears
    and in our hearts,
    to walk in your way.
Not only with our lips,
    but in our lives,
    we give you glory.

146   Why do you stand so far off, Lord,
          hiding your face
          when we most need to see you?
      Come to us now, Lord.
      Show us the light of your countenance,
          your peace.
      Lord, speak to us,
          your people are waiting.

147   We build our altars in one place, Lord.
      These hearts ready,
          these lives dedicated to your word.
      This people present.
      This sacrament prepared.
      This message of comfort,
          waiting to be given.
      We build our altars in one place, Lord.
      Send down your fire upon us,
          as you will:
          wherever you will.

148   Your Church has made many mistakes, Lord.
      Help her not to add to them
          by making the last mistake of all,
          and ceasing to exist.
      Help us to cling to your word, Lord.
      Help us to cling to each other.
      Help us to build
          on your foundations only.

This world is for forgiving other people, Lord,   *149*
   when they hurt us,
   when they neglect us.
Eternity is for forgiving ourselves,
   knowing that we are this moment
   and every moment totally loved,
   totally understood, totally forgiven.
We bring our own sins before you, Lord.
You know what they are, who we are.
You stretch out your hand toward us,
   and we are healed.

We are not worthy, Lord,   *150*
   to approach your table.
And yet we are worthy,
   your Spirit makes us so,
   your love poured into our hearts.
We confess our sins, Lord,
   those ways not taken.
That way of love and sacrifice
   not followed.
We confess to you our sins.
But we confess our faith also.
Your love for us above all,
   comforts us, refreshes us,
   renews us, heals us.
Lord, I am not worthy.
But you are.

151   Inside every sinner, Lord,
       there is a saint waiting to get out.
    Inside every broken soul,
       a mended spirit waiting to be whole.
    In our lives also,
       you are always with us.
    No besetting sin can keep you away.
    You who are our friend always.

152   We confess our sins, Lord,
       to you and before each other.
    The things we have left undone.
    The things done wrongly.
    Paths not taken.
    The path turned away from.
    You never leave us, Lord,
       however far we stray.
    Your love calls us back.
    We confess our sins to you,
       who love us and are with us always.

153   Forgive us our sins, Lord,
       those things we have done wrongly,
       those good things we have not done,
       that good path we have not taken.
    Help us to do better, Lord,
       in our trusting of you
       to help us and redeem us.
    May our hearts and minds be filled
       with your goodness,
       not our own weakness.
    Come to us, Lord, now, today.
    When we are lowly in our own eyes,
       you lift us up.

We kneel before you, Lord.   *154*
Not what we are now,
    but what we shall be.
Not where we are now,
    but where your Spirit will lead us.
We kneel with your Son Jesus
    before the possibilities
    of our own lives also.

We confess our sins, Lord,   *155*
    but also our virtues.
Those things we have done well,
    those good things we tried to be,
    even if we failed.
We confess our faith, Lord,
    before each other
    and in our own hearts,
    that you come to us as a people,
    but also one by one.
You bless us, sustain us, forgive us.
Give us your peace.

We confess our sins to you, Lord,   *156*
    but also to each other.
The state of the world is our fault.
We are all to blame,
    but only partly to blame.
Our sins and our virtues are inherited in part.
We influence each other for good or evil.
Help our prayer for each other.
We bring you our sins, Lord,
    of thought, word and deed.
Our lives are open to you.
We await your blessing.

157   Be merciful to our sins, Lord,
        for they are great.
    But your love for us is greater.
    Speedily you come to us,
        stop your donkey on the road
        where we have fallen,
        pour in your own oil and wine,
        carry us to your inn,
        help us to continue our journey.
    You are our journey, Lord,
        but also our companion on the way.

158   On the night of your betrayal, Lord,
        your gave us your own self,
        your own Spirit,
        though we betray you
        and do not understand.
    Through our betrayal, you come to us.
    Give us your love,
        the bread your hand has broken,
        the wine your life has blessed.
    We receive you, Lord,
        the forgiveness of your love.
    Your Spirit comes to us.

159   You so love the world, Lord,
        you so love your people,
        your servants, each one of us,
        that you give us your own Son,
        to be our friend,
        to die for us daily,
        to bring us life.
    Come to us now.

Father, send your Spirit,
   make clean our hearts
   to love you and hear you.
We confess our sins which so trouble us,
   so burden us, hinder our race
   in running the way of your command.

Our sins of thought, we humbly confess.   *160*
Of cowardice, of boldness without thought.
We confess our sins,
   of things done or said
   against your word.
Of things not done or said
   to assist your kingdom.
We confess our faith, our trust in you,
   who absolve us.
Embrace us, cherish us,
   and never condemn.
Now and in eternity.

We bring before you our sins, Lord,   *161*
   but also our virtues.
Those graces and gifts
   your love has given us.
Opportunities to serve you,
   help us to use them wisely.
Opportunities to love you
   in the brothers and sisters
   your love affords us today.

We confess our sins to God but also our faith.
If our heart condemns us,
God is greater than our heart and knows all things.

162 It does not yet appear, Lord,
   what we shall be.
 Your love sees what we are now,
   but also what we shall become
   by your star's leading.
 Shine on us, Lord.
 Shine through us, to your heart's content.
 Save us.
 Bless your people.
 Save all your children.
 Save the world.

163 You turn our water into wine, Lord.
 Our lives are not ordinary
   to you who made us,
   and die for us daily.
 Hour by hour, day by day,
   all our life long
   you pass your hand over
   our ordinary lives.
 And we are ordinary no longer.
 We are your wine, Lord,
   fruit of your vineyard.
 You are the vine,
   and we are the branches.
 Day by day,
   you tend us and nourish us.

164 Bread and wine, unite us to each other.
 Make us one family
   for the world's healing,
   our own redemption.
 Bread and wine, link us to Jesus,

unite us to him first of all.
For whoever finds true love is alive.
Whoever finds love
   is united to the whole world.

We will sing of your love, Lord,   *165*
   for all your children.
Living and departed,
   all souls in the world's history,
   here in this moment of time.
We offer our prayers to you,
   our lives to you
   for the sake of others,
   that your kingdom
   may come in us.
With bread and wine,
   we set forth
   the life of your Son Jesus.

Our cup overflows, Lord,   *166*
   with the opportunity your love offers.
We break the bread of sorrows
   as well as life.
You come to us in this feast,
   this recollection of your love for us,
   your rescuing of us in all dangers.
Come to us now, Lord,
   come to us again,
   never leave us.
Come to us now in the life of your Son.

167   Mary and Joseph, pray for us,
        as we prepare your Son's feast.
Celebrate his life in bread and wine,
        as the Father begs us,
        so we come together.
We proclaim his death upon the cross,
        his death for us.
His life in us always.

168   We gather around your table, Lord.
We are your people,
        your community,
        made so by your Spirit.
We offer you ourselves.
But ourselves as you see us
        and not as the world does.
Do not look upon our sins, Lord,
        but look on our faith.
Brothers and sisters of your Son Jesus,
        we meet in his name.
We offer our lives to you in him.

169   The table is laid, Lord.
Your table.
This bread, made by our hands.
This wine, symbol of our life,
        and of our nationhood.
Members of your family,
        each one of us a branch on your vine,
        giving forth fruit.
Come to us, Lord.
Prune our minds of all unclear thoughts,
        help us to give you glory.

The table is set, Lord. *170*
Your people are gathered.
Each one in our own place
    around your table.
Each one having our own place
    in your kingdom.
And yet there are more here
    than we can see or greet.
Our friends who have died
    worship you in glory.
We pray with them and they with us.

We recall your Son's birth, Lord, *171*
    but also our own.
We recall his death,
    show forth his love again.
To the world, he is dead.
His life in vain,
    his words of forgiveness have no meaning.
But to us they are life.
The chance to start again.
To us he is alive for ever.

Your whole people praise you, Lord. *172*
Young and old,
    rich and poor,
    one with another.
We are all rich in your word, Lord.
In your estimation of us,
    of our calling.
We meet each other around your table.
We meet you in the bread and wine.
We meet you in each other.

173   Morning by morning you waken us
         to hear your word.
      Your Son speaks to us.
      Your Spirit comes to us.
      Kindling in us hopes
         we did not know we had.
      Dreams we never knew we possessed.
      Your Spirit makes us a people, Lord.
      Your people, united by your Spirit.
      Speak to us, Lord,
         in the bread's breaking,
         and in each other.
      Your love is sufficient, Lord,
         for all our needs.
      We gather up your manna daily,
         enough for this day,
         enough for this hour,
         but no more.
      Tomorrow we will see your love again,
         fresh for our new needs.
      Dear Lord, you come to us daily.

      Heal us, cleanse us, mend us.
      Bind our fractured parts together
         in your unity, your peace.
      Come to us, Lord,
         come to us now,
         as a garden ready to be watered,
         your servants are waiting.

174   We recall your Son's death and resurrection,
         his death on the cross,
         his brief life on earth,
         for our sakes.
      We tell forth his resurrection in us.

It is Christmas, Lord,   *175*
    and we do not celebrate
    your Son's birth only:
    but every son,
    every daughter.
While the Emperor counts everybody
    in his empire,
    you count us your friends.
While the Emperor proclaims:
    count everybody,
    your love announces:
    everybody counts.
We count,
    who belong to
    your empire also.

Today is Pentecost, Lord.   *176*
Your people are renewed
    and created again,
    by the coming of your Spirit.
Come to us again, Lord,
    enable us to praise you
    with many voices,
    each one our own.
But help us to proclaim your love
    with one heart,
    one mind,
    one voice,
    in a language everyone can understand.

The Prayer of Consecration and the Communion

177   *That same day two of them were on their way to a village called Emmaus, about seven miles from Jerusalem . . . As they talked with one another Jesus himself came up and walked beside them, but something held their eyes from knowing who it was . . . And when they had sat down at the table, he took the bread and blessed it . . .*
Luke 24:13-30

It is never easy to pinpoint the exact moment in any celebration of the sacrament when Jesus himself starts to walk beside us, and the congregation of two, or a hundred and two, is increased by one.

Jesus is always walking beside us, though we may not feel conscious of his presence, or realise till much later those people or apparently trivial moments through which he spoke.

Most celebrations end with our going back the way we have come, to lives and people that may appear exactly the same as when we left home. Yet they are not quite the same. For we can tell them 'we have seen the Lord'.

If not with our lips then in our lives, we will give him glory.

'Preach the gospel to every creature, use words if necessary.' (St Francis of Assisi)

Lord, hear this Mass we offer.   *178*
When I am poor and neglected,
  and all the doors of society are closed against me,
  you come to me in my stable.
You find me a home,
  you send your shepherds to call me by name,
  keep watch over me.
Your wise men arrive,
  our living will not be in vain.
To earth's farthest bounds
  will the effects of my life be felt.
You give me your gifts.
Lonely on my cross, you come to me.
Broken in my grave,
  you roll back the stone, declare I am alive.
Lord, we offer this Mass to you,
  in union with your Son Jesus.
We are broken and alone,
  but your Spirit sustains us and lifts us up.
We offer you our lives,
  we are risen with Christ,
  we live to your glory.

As often as we break this bread,   *179*
  we show your life again.
As often as we drink this cup,
  we show your death and resurrection.
Your Son's death is our life, Lord,
  his resurrection is our own.
Sunday by Sunday
  we come to the tomb
  and see no sign of death,
  only of love's triumph,
  and our own calling and renewal.

180   We do this in remembrance of you, Lord,
      who brought your people out of slavery,
      who bring us out of bondage and servitude,
      out of darkness into light,
      out of sin and dereliction to serve you in glory.
    You are our friend, Lord.
    Father before us,
      Son beside us,
      Spirit within us.
    You never leave us.
    You bring us to your kingdom.

181   We meet in your Son's name,
      beneath the shadow of his cross.
    To the world it was defeat,
      to us it is victory.
    To the world failure,
      to us the triumph of your love.
    We proclaim this life, Lord,
      we set it forth in bread and wine.
    A meal for all your children,
      each of us welcomed at your table.
    This is your body, Lord,
      this people here,
      met in your name,
      eating the bread of your new covenant,
      love's kingdom on earth established.
    This is your blood, Lord,
      this is your life, flowing in our veins,
      one for another,
      this life poured out
      for all of us,
      to heal us, renew us,
      bring us to your kingdom.

This is your body, Lord,   *182*
   this bread we share.
This is your life, your blood
   shed for us, given for us,
   this cup we drink.
We are your body, Lord,
   alive by your grace;
   your Spirit only
   enlivens us,
   gives us your peace.

Take the cup now, Lord.   *183*
Take it again.
Bless it.
Turn the water of our lives into wine.
Turn the water of our suffering
   into life for the world.
Come to us now, Lord.
Your people are waiting.

This is your body, Lord,   *184*
   but also our own.
Our own lives broken,
   offered in your service,
   shared with each other.
This is your cup, Lord,
   but also our own.
Your blood flows in our veins,
   assists us, gives us life.
We cannot drink your cup, Lord,
   you drank that for us years ago.
And yet we do drink your cup,
   and make your life our own,
   each of us for the other.

185   Our hearts are open to your word, Lord.
You know our need of you
    before we ask.
Our weaknesses
    before we confess them,
    our failures in your word,
    our doors so firmly fastened
    against your love.
Come to us now, Lord,
    heal us, save us.
We are your servants,
    your vessels,
    waiting to be filled.

186   We recall your Son's death, Lord,
    the night he was betrayed.
He took bread and blessed it
    that we might eat.
Took wine and poured it,
    that we might receive his life.
This is his body,
    given for us.
This is his blood,
    for all his people shed.
We recall your Son's death, dear Father.
We receive his resurrection
    but also our own.

187   We offer you this bread and wine.
Is it not the body of your Son?
His life for us,
    your love for us in him.
Are we not his body,
    his people also?

This wine we drink,
   is it not his life,
   your life,
   flowing in our veins?
We drink it to your glory.

There is no holy communion, Lord,   *188*
   without holy community.
Help us to belong to your family first.
Your ancient people, the Jews,
   renewed and refreshed
   by the life and death
   of your servant Jesus.
In him, we are all renewed.
By your Spirit,
   we all share his resurrection.
Help us to tell your story, Lord,
   to all peoples in all lands.
Beginning here,
   beginning now

We proclaim the life of your Son, Lord,   *189*
   here at this table
   as his life demands of us.
The bread set out,
   that all may feed.
The cup of affliction,
   but also joy,
   from which we drink.
We offer our lives to you, Lord,
   in union with his own.
Christ in us,
   Messiah in each one of us.
Your love for each of us continuously.

190   Set us up upon the rock
        that is higher than we are.
    You are our rock, Lord,
      we build our lives on you.
    Without you, we can do nothing.
    By your grace, we can do everything.
    There is no limit
        to your grace in our own lives.
    Come to us now, Lord.
    Cleanse us, refresh us, help us.
    Assist us by your grace to start again.

191   We meet in your name, Lord,
        but also in our own.
    You give us our name
      in the waters of baptism,
      in the water of our tears,
      as we repent,
      turn back toward you daily.
    Love is your name, Lord,
      sacrifice for us is your meaning.
    We offer our own lives also,
      in this bread and in this wine,
      each of us given for the other.

192   We show forth your death, Lord.
    To the world it is defeat
      but to us victory.
    To the world it is life's ending,
      to us resurrection.
    To the world failure,
      to us love and victory beyond comparison.
    We show forth your death, Lord.
    We proclaim our own resurrection.

Where there is hatred,
   let us sow love.
Where there is injury,
   pardon.
Where there is despair,
   hope.
Here at this table, Lord,
   to which your love invites us,
   we set forth and proclaim
   the life of your Son.
Where there is war,
   let there be peace,
   through this life
   which we together
   proclaim and share.

193

We break this bread, Lord,
   to share it with each other.
Your Son's life given freely
   to each one of us.
When we are blind,
   you help us to see.
When we are deaf
   to love's entreaties,
   you speak to us.
When we are dumb,
   you touch our lips
   to sing your praises,
   communicate your love.

194

195   We drink to your health, Lord,
        but also to our own.
    And to the world's salvation.
    We eat this bread of affliction
        but also life.
    Food to sustain us
        in our wanderings
        and in our uncertainty.
    We offer you our lives,
        in union with your Son Jesus.
    We proclaim his life to all the world
        but in your love
        and in your name first of all.

The Gloria

196   *. . . and suddenly there was with the Angel a multitude of the heavenly host praising God and saying, 'Glory to God in the highest and on earth peace, good will to his people on earth.'*
Luke 2:13-14

None of us can be thinking or praying all the time. We would get exhausted. There is a place for praising only, and giving glory: and resting in God or life, rather than asking things of it. There is a place for listening to someone else's song and joining in a tune we did not have to labour to compose. And yet the tune belongs to us also. We are all part of God's symphony. The note or notes sounded by our lives are each one quite distinctive. 'The Lord loves to hear his crows as well as his nightingales.'

Glory be to God on high,   *197*
   and on the earth his peace.
With angels and archangels
   we praise his holy name.
With shepherds in the field,
   blinded by the light of God's love,
   we kneel and adore him.

Glory to you, Lord,   *198*
   in the morning and in the evening.
Glory to you, when we are young.
Glory, when we are old.
All the stages of our life give you glory.
All the stages of this day.
In the morning and in the evening,
   we praise your holy name.

We recall your Son's death, Lord.   *199*
We show it forth proudly.
We proclaim it.
That to die in poverty,
   all the world condemning,
   this is true wealth.
That to die alone,
   everyone neglecting you,
   no one understanding,
   this is true company.
That to die forgiving,
   speaking kindly to those
   who handed you over,
   this is true life.
And the world's renewal.

200   Dear Lord, we praise you.
      With bread that human hands have made
          to give us life.
      And give you glory.
      With wine that human hands have poured,
          grapes of your vine,
          pressed down and running over.
      Our cup is full, Lord,
          to overflowing,
          with all your goodness for us.
      In the life of your Son Jesus,
          we give you glory.

201   You make the morning and the night, Lord.
      One follows the other,
          each in its proper place
          gives you glory.
      The night for sleeping,
          secure in your love.
      The day for service,
          as well as we may.
      Each in our own place
          we give you glory.

202   We give you glory, Lord,
          as the first shepherds did
          who celebrated your birth,
          kept watch over you.
      We give you glory, Lord,
          for your care of us,

your watching over
   our souls' needs day by day.
We give you glory for our lives also.
In our own lives
   and in our deaths we praise you.
In your own life,
   and in your Son's death,
   we find resurrection.

We trust in you, Lord,   *203*
   but also in ourselves.
What you have done in us,
   what you will do.
Your plans for us are good, Lord.
For love's purpose only
   are we formed,
   to serve you,
   to serve others in you,
   to be loved by you for ever.

We are your people, Lord,   *204*
   you have chosen us.
By the sea of Galilee
   we heard your word.
When we were in our own homes,
   you saw us and called us.
When we worked at our fishing nets,
   or counted the gifts you had given us,
   you spoke to us saying
   love is the greatest gift of all.

205   Come, Lord, in this communion.
Come, Lord, in this community.
We are a people, first of all.
Your people, even when
    two or three are present.
We are your people,
    met in your name,
    called by your Spirit,
    waiting for instruction.
Dear Lord, we praise you.

206   Help us to hear the meaning of your life, Lord.
Your love for us,
    your care for all your children.
It is better to be born in ignominy
    than to leave others outside
    to live in the stable.
It is better to preach your word
    than to ignore its kindness,
    better to die in desolation
    than curse those who hate us.
Better to rise again on the third day
    in love's name, and no one else's.
Dear Lord, we give you glory.

207   Let us be glad and rejoice in your friendship, Lord.
You who have made us,
    and brought us safely to this day.
Through trials and tribulations
    you support us,
    you never leave us,
    however far we wander

from your word, your ways.
Come to us now, Lord.
Bless us, refresh us, revive us.
We rejoice in your friendship,
    and in our own.

We hold up our hands to you in prayer,   *208*
    we hold up our lives.
The five fingers and two hands
    your love has lent us.
The five loaves and two fishes
    your love has given us,
    with which to praise you
    and feed the world.
We hold up our lives to you, Lord,
    we wait for your blessing.
In your time and by your Spirit
    may the world be fed.

We are your people, Lord.   *209*
Bread baked by your mother's hand,
    kneaded and made ready
    to feed a hungry world.
We are your vineyard, Lord.
You are the gardener.
We are the vine,
    each one of us a branch,
    nourished by your love,
    your dying for us daily.
You are the vine.
We are the branches.
Each of us in our own way,
    grows to your glory.

210   We drink your cup, Lord,
       your life flows in our veins.
    We eat this bread
      of your affliction
      and our own.
    For forty years your people travelled,
      seeking rest.
    You bring us to the kingdom, Lord,
      we enter Jerusalem.
    This is the promised land.

211   We pray for your Church, Lord,
      near and far,
      here and now,
      for our own lives also.
    For the peace of the whole world,
      for your peace
      in our own country.
    For those who suffer
      in body, mind or spirit,
        through hunger, thirst or loneliness,
      who suffer oppression.
    You have made of one blood
      all nations of the earth
      to live in harmony.
    Living and departed,
      Lord, we praise you,
      we adore you.

212   We believe in your Church, Lord.
    Despite all our sins,
      you inhabit us,
      influence us,
      bring us to our journey's end.

The boat launched at Galilee
   is still travelling,
   still at work.
There is room in her for all your children.
Each of us has our own place,
   beside the lobster pots
   and Andrew's fishing tackle.
Peter and Andrew, pray for us.
Paul and Barnabas, inspire us.
Mary and Joseph,
   protect us by your grace.
It is your Church, Lord,
   though the waves are rough.
You speak to us from her.
Your Spirit inspires us,
   leads us forward.

Departing

Not for these alone do I pray,   213
but for those who will believe through them.
John 17:20

When Jesus first fed five thousand people with the five loaves and two small fishes, all that life had given him, he asked his disciples to gather up the fragments that remained, so that nothing would be lost. We have been doing it ever since.

Only so many people can come to any particular celebration. But when we go out of God's house we do not go out of his presence. All the people we meet are members of his family, if not immediately of ours. We pray for them, and wish them well. That they may be blessed and fed by God's love also.

Not for us alone does Jesus pray. But for those who will believe, through us.

214   Defend us, Lord.
You are our shield,
   the rock on which we build,
   our shelter in the storm.
We rest in your word.
We rest in each other.
We go out in the power of your Spirit,
   to love you and serve you.

215   Let nothing be lost, Lord,
   gather up the fragments that remain,
   of this feast, of our own lives.
Nothing is ever wasted, Lord,
   those things we have forgotten,
   those people who have passed
   through our lives.
We offer ourselves to you, Lord,
   our future is safe in your hands.
We love you and serve you today.

216   We will do great things through you, Lord.
Greater than you did,
   because you are with us.
More than you did,
   for you were one and we are many.
Yet you are many in us, Lord,
   through us.
Your work is our work,
   your life is ours,
   now and for ever.

We are your body, Lord,   *217*
   nourished by your feast.
We love you, we serve you.

To you be the glory, Lord,   *218*
   in our own lives.
To you be the power,
   for you are our strength.
To you be our prayer,
   for you are our love,
   our hope, our stay.

We pray for your Church, Lord,   *219*
   in all lands and in all places.
We are your Church, Lord,
   ready to serve you.
We pray for your Church, Lord,
   all ages in a moment of time,
   our friends departed
   in your love and care.
They are safe, Lord,
   they join their praises to ours.
They encourage us, pray for us.
Mary and Joseph, your servants,
   pray for us daily.

220   We set our hope on you, Lord.
        You are our strength, and our song.
        You are the story that we tell,
            day by day.
        You are our friend in the past,
            love recorded,
            love told again daily.
        You are our hope in the future,
            no one else knowing,
            no one else caring
            as you do.
        You are our hope and strength
            today and always.

221   You are the well of our life, Lord.
        A deep well, filled with water.
        Of your love for us,
            there is no end.
        The more we drink from your cup,
            the more there is to drink.
        Like life-giving waters,
            you refresh us and cleanse us,
            and feed us.
        It is a new day, a new beginning.

222   You are our strength, Lord,
            our life and our song.
        Daily we speak of your goodness,
            your loving kindness to all your children.
        We tell your story,
            day by day we tell of your goodness.
        With our lips and with our lives
            we serve and obey you.

We believe in you, Lord,   *223*
    but also in ourselves.
We are your servants, Lord,
    waiting on your word.
Your breath in our lungs,
    your life in our hearts.
One by one we serve you,
    each in our own way,
    we give you glory.
We lose ourselves in your love for us.
We lose ourselves but find ourselves,
    in this community
    which gives you praise.

We do not look for your second coming, Lord,   *224*
    we are content with your first.
Here and now you save us,
    come to us,
    bless us,
    sustain us.
Give us strength when we are weary,
    enable us to rest in your love,
    enable us to run
    in the way of love's command.
Even so, Lord Jesus,
    come quickly.

We ask you to do more   *225*
    in our lives, Lord,
    that we may do less.
Relying on your friendship for us,
    your words of encouragement,

spoken daily,
   dwelt on at leisure.
We feed on your word, Lord.
We feed on the life of your Son,
   expressed in this fellowship,
   each one of us praying for the other.

226   You do not give us what we deserve, Lord,
   but what we need.
Your love, your kindness,
   your understanding,
   your forgiveness.
Out of nothing
   you create us daily.
Each moment is the gift of your love,
   the world preventing you,
   the world getting in your way.
Our hearts are fixed on you only, Lord.
You who love us unreservedly.

227   Dear Lord, hear my prayer.
Though I am born in a stable,
   and all the doors of society
   are closed against me,
   you send me your shepherds
   to watch over me,
   and call me by name.
Wise men from the east arrive,
   at your bidding alone,
   to say that my obscure birth
   will yet influence and affect
   all the world.

And though I die in loneliness,
   no one understanding,
   and am buried in another's tomb
   with no prayers said
   to speed my journey.
Yet will you send your messengers
   to roll back the stone
   and call me back, saying to the world:
   I am alive for ever.

Our spirits rise to greet you, Lord.   *228*
We wait on your word.
Like birds in the sky,
   we rest on your wind.
Like fishes in the sea,
   we swim in the ocean of your love.
Our lives are limited
   to this time and place.
Your love for us is limitless.
Like the stars in the sky,
   and the sand on the sea shore,
   so shall the opportunities of this day
   afford you glory.

Do not hide your face from us, Lord.   *229*
Show us your love,
   but also your purposes.
Give us your peace,
   but also your work to do,
   our own duties to perform.
Give us your love, Lord,
   that we may give to others,
   love others,
   for your Son's sake only.

230 May your name be kept holy, Lord.
Your meaning for us, in the world.
Your love for the world,
 which never changes.
For if we remain true to your name, Lord,
 your kingdom will come.
And where your kingdom is,
 there may our hearts be always.

231 Not only with our lips but with our life,
 here in this place,
 one with another,
 your whole Church is present,
 praying and believing.
Living and departed,
 young and old,
 each of us contributing our own part
 to your praises.
Not only with our lips
 but with our lives,
 we will serve you.

232 Not only with our lips, Lord,
 but with our lives,
 we will praise you.
Not only with this bread and wine,
 not only with these prayers and hymns,
 but all our lives in every part
 tell out your story.

Praying in the Darkness

It is bad enough being low in spirit without having   233
the burden of religion to make it worse. Religion is
the preserve of those who try to do better and so
necessarily fail, and feel under condemnation.

But the attempt to do well is itself the chief glory
and triumph. 'Well done, good and faithful servant',
for trying and failing.

The best priests or Christians tend to be those who
are older. They have failed most. People cling to Peter
the first Pope (if he was that) because he was fallible.
Not faultless.

Beginnings

Welcome to the rest of my life, Lord.   234
The first day of it.
It may be the only one.
Were there other days?
If so, you have forgiven them.
Will there be other days to come?
If so, they are your responsibility.
But here and now,
    I open the door
    and welcome you,
    friend of my darkest moments,
    friend in my despair.

235   I'm glad you are not a psychiatrist, Lord.
Trying to understand me,
    unravel me,
    make sense of my life's
    complicated mechanisms.
You do more than understand me,
    you love me.
Reaching deep into my heart,
    you give me meaning.
No, I may not be 'normal'. Who is?
No, I may not be 'balanced'.
But I am myself,
    and in my complexities you love me.

236   You called us by name, Lord,
    before we called you.
Outside the tomb,
    in darkness of soul.
    In the failure of our lives
    you called us your rock,
    salt of the earth,
    light of the world,
    although we ourselves felt dark.
We were called Christians, Lord,
    before you were.
Jesus, my unknown friend, love me.

237   For God has chosen us,
    the depressives of this world,
    to comfort the happy.
He has chosen us,

who have no sense of our own value,
to give other lives meaning.
He has chosen the lowly vessels
to lift others high,
the dirtied cups
to wash and refresh others.
In my brokenness, Lord,
I give you glory.

Help me to use the sufferings I've got, Lord.   *238*
I shan't, after all, be able
to offer them to you for ever.
They are unique.
No one else has them, thankfully.
No one else knows you
in quite the way I do.
This burden is all my own.
Yet all your own, always.

Do you take your life with or without wine?   *239*
I suppose, Lord, we should do both.
Accept the wine offered to us on our cross,
any comfort, any blessing,
any alleviation of our soul's pain.
That which will help us bear our cross,
be borne on it,
no one else quite understanding.
And yet in a way we cannot drink it.
Our own life is our own gift,
burden, terror.
Help us, dear Lord,

to accept all the consolations
life has to offer.
But to decline that one consolation
of no longer being ourselves,
ceasing to be ourselves.
You love us, Lord.
You suffer with us, hold us up.

240   We are all in prison, Lord,
of one sort or another,
and no one knows,
no one sees the bars,
hemming me in,
keeping life and opportunity out.
Nobody sees, Lord, except you.
You look at me as a father
looks at his child,
new born in a cruel world.
You keep watch over me,
and release me, daily.

241   Now I see you, Lord, now I don't.
Sometimes you are there,
usually not.
And in darkness I go on,
chiselling out my life painfully
from this solid block of stone, so unyielding.
I chip away slowly, Lord.
A pattern slowly emerges,
not seen until the end.
One day you will see the finished work,
and be well satisfied with it.

This prayer, Lord, is for those   *242*
    who find life a handicap.
A burden, not an opportunity.
A sentence to be endured,
    a day to be got through somehow.
Please bless my handicap, Lord.
    I may be doing better than I know.
Please bless my burden.
    I may be carrying more than I realise.

No doubt you love me, Lord,   *243*
    but I cannot experience your love.
No doubt the sun shines,
    but it does not warm my soul.
The rain falls,
    but does not refresh those deep parts of me
    only your brokenness can touch.
So I cling to your cross, Lord,
    though I'd rather have your resurrection.

Help me to use the sins I have, Lord.   *244*
I won't get the chance
    to fail in this way again.
And if I do, I'll be older,
    more grateful for your forgiveness.

245   It says in the book, Lord, that you love me.
But I do not experience this love,
    have no feeling of it.
Other people ask, 'How are you?'
And I am not able to answer.
Dully, and in pain, I go on slowly.
Like you, I find the wine offered
    on my cross cannot help.
For I am totally alone.
And yet, on the way to my cross,
    I accept such solaces as the world affords.
Weep for the world, Lord.
And, in your mercy, save us.

246   Stop the world, Lord,
    I want to get on.
Breathe again my first breath.
Start again my first steps.
Hear again the first words ever said to me.
Son, daughter,
    I love you.

247   I wish I was dead, Lord.
    But this is not strictly true.
I wish my sufferings were dead,
    I wish the blackness of my mind would disperse.
But since it has not dispersed,
    I keep my hand in the hand
    of one I cannot feel,
    and thank you that I have managed thus far.
And do I wish I was dead?
Say, rather, I wish I was alive.

Dear Lord, I will carry any cross you like,   *248*
   provided it is not my own.
I find my own weaknesses so hard to bear;
   my own failure; my own depression.
And yet, as well as I may,
   I offer my life to you.
I ask you to bless it if you can,
   in ways I may never know.
I ask you to use my failure, my breakdown,
   to help others in their quest for faith.
Dear Lord, I offer my life and my failures to you,
   to be a blessing for others.
In your way and in your time,
   please use me, for Jesus' sake.

For comfort's sake

Though Jesus of Nazareth was not a doctor, those   *249*
who met him tended to feel better, whatever their
age. His friendship was his treatment. And those
who only touched the outskirts of his life found
themselves standing straighter and taller than
before.

St Luke, himself a medical man, gives us the most
personal gospel. And, being a doctor, he knew the
value of family ties and upbringing in Jesus' own
life. He begins his gospel with the family then, Jesus'
aunt and uncle, Elizabeth and Zachariah. And how
they named their child John (the Baptist), though
no one in their family had had that name before.
None of us, they were saying, is a recycled edition
of his parents. We all have our own unique name
and meaning.

So Jesus welcomes us to this new day; We are

ourselves, and quite unique in God's perception of us. Our sufferings and experiences and triumphs are unique also.

250   I change houses, Lord, but never my home.
My true home is in your word daily, your love.
I change jobs, but never that one work
    of chiselling away at your likeness.
I change friends.
Imperceptibly they drift away,
    faces mingle in the crowd,
    disappear, reappear.
But you are always there, smiling.

251   Listen to my words, Lord.
Especially those I am too shy to utter,
    even to myself.
Listen to my hopes,
    even those I never knew I had.
Listen to my fears,
    those I cannot describe,
    only experience.
Above all, Lord, beneath all this,
    listen to me.

252   You set me at liberty, Lord.
You give me freedom.
Touch the deep parts of my soul,
    unleash new energies, new possibilities,
    new worlds for my soul to visit.
And yet I live in one world only.
Your world.
Your kingdom.

Slowly it changes,
    or I change in it.
You lead me to new countries,
    beyond the map.

You turn water into wine, Lord.   *253*
Most people seem to turn wine
    back into water.
The world takes my best endeavours,
    my attempts at goodness,
    and belittles them,
    makes small of them.
But you magnify my virtues,
    make great my littleness.
Stretching out your hand
    over the ordinariness of this day,
    you bless it.
You bless me.

Here I stand, Lord,   *254*
    with a world to be fed.
My two hands held up to you,
    five fingers on each.
My two loaves and five fishes,
    all I have with a world to be fed.
But you take my contribution
    to the world's need.
You hold it high,
    hold me high.
You give thanks for my life,
    and my actions this day.
However small, they travel outward
    till the world is fed.

255   When I was a child,
          I thought as a child,
          spoke as a child.
      But when I grew up in your word,
          the world got stuck to my fingers.
      But I never lost my childhood, Lord,
          so far as you are concerned.
      Wherever I go, whatever happens,
          I am still your little one,
          the servant you delight in.

256   Help me to keep my eyes, Lord,
          on the road in front.
      Yes, I have to check in the rear mirror.
      Where I have been is important.
      It led me to where I am now.
      There are always cars trying to overtake,
          those whose lives have more horsepower,
          whose feet are constantly on the pedal.
      And yes, there are always those
          who will be ahead of me, faster.
      But, such as I am, I am coming.

257   You bless our mistakes, Lord, as well as our virtues.
      Sometimes our mistakes are the best part of us.
      Leading us to positions from which
          your love can rescue us,
          enable us, assist us,
          in a new way.
      Help me to do my best, Lord.
          But not better than my best.

Help me not to push the issue, or my health,
    further than they can go.
It's your world, Lord,
    your responsibility.
Don't rub out my mistakes.
Weave them in.

You see the life I try to live,   *258*
    inside the life I live.
You take me to new pastures.
Enable me to gallop.
Discover new parts of my soul
    I never knew existed.
I was happy in that ignorance!
But now I am older, Lord,
    and if I don't feel wiser,
    you at least never leave me.
You touch those parts of me
    other prophets cannot reach.

You are my defender, Lord.   *259*
You lift up my head,
    and pour in oil and wine
    to those deep wounds life has left.
Your water cleanses me.
You set me on your own beast.
You walk beside me to the inn.
You help me walk again,
    in my own time,
    at my own pace.
The future belongs to you also.

260 My other car is a Jaguar, Lord.
My other dog a Rottweiler.
My other wife or husband a film star.
But you are concerned
 with the life I have, Lord,
 this day ahead of me,
 this moment now.
You specialise in the actual,
 as well as the impossible.
You are the God of those whose feet
 are caked in mud,
 while their heads are in the skies.

261 The world is my oyster, Lord,
 and not my hospital.
And if it is my hospital
 I get out of bed while no one is looking.
And in spirit at least move nearer the door.
You are my visitor, at all hours,
 not only those appointed.
My doctor on call, constantly.
My strength, my hope, my friend.

262 I never was any good at heights, Lord.
Looking down from the theologians' lofty position.
The angels' position, who give you glory.
I am more at home at the crib,
 looking over the wooden edges.
I notice amid the straw,
 the ox and ass gazing at me.
Expecting great things.
They still do.
You are very particular who you visit, Lord.
You visit me.

I love my wife, Lord,   263
    though I am not married.
My brother and sister,
    though I am an only child.
My mother and father,
    though they left home years ago.
The world is your family, Lord.
This one person I meet today
    belongs to me also.
I am never alone

It's not that I worry more, Lord.   264
Just that I have more to worry with.
More years, more failures, more bruises.
These I carry with me.
They are my scars, my battle medals
    worn by me unwillingly for you,
    who worry about me!

It takes twenty-two years to be twenty-two, Lord.   265
You can't hurry it.
Pull at the flowers in your garden
    to make them grow faster,
    us grow faster.
One day I'll outgrow
    the wayward impulses of youth.
Move over to the middle lane,
    then the slow one, on life's motorway.
One day I'll stop altogether.
Get out and enjoy the view,
    your view.
Till then, at my own speed,
    I journey onward.

266   My heart is fixed, Lord.
      And no, I've not got arthritis.
   My heart is rooted only
      in a love that never changes,
      a faith in me that never alters,
      a hope for my future as well as my past,
      that both may be blessed.
   My hope is in you only, Lord.
   My faith and love are in you alone.
   My heart is rooted and grounded
      in your love.

267   I possess the world, Lord,
      its farthest places.
   Though I am confined
      to one small life,
      one particular moment
      in the world's time.
   Yet my Spirit soars.
   Beneath my frail body,
      beneath the burdens of my soul,
      beneath my mind, even,
      you are there.
   You never leave me.

268   Though I am born outside society
      you come to me in my stable.
   Though my life is not accepted
      in the synagogue or the inn,
      still you watch over me
      and are my friend.

Though I die on the cross,
   condemned by all the gods,
   and all the doors of society
   remain closed to my presence,
   and though I am buried
   in a borrowed tomb,
   with no chance of ceremony,
   still you wait with me,
   and send angels to roll back the stone.
You say I am alive.

Day by day

The chief difficulty for religious people is not whether   *269*
God exists, but whether we do. Jesus affirmed the
value of each person he met, finding faith in the most
unexpected places. He did not go about saying, 'I am
the Christ', but helped other people to feel they were.

Zacchaeus was so small he had to climb a tree to
feel ten feet tall. Mary of Magdala was given her
name back, and known by her name 'Mary', not by
her town or supposed occupation.

But what if Zacchaeus climbed his tree because
Jesus was a small man and got lost in the crowds?
We are not given any indication of Jesus' appearance
or habits, only those of his cousin John. But Jesus
may have been a small man in one way. Like all
prophets and healers he looked up to other people
and made them feel taller.

As he does to us today. Looking at us and smiling
and saying: Great is our faith.

270   Dear Lord, day by day you name me,
        give my life meaning.
    There will never be another 'me'
        in all history.
    The circumstances of my life may be common,
        may be depressed.
    But I am of such value to you, Lord.
    You begin your gospel
        with your own personal shepherd
        checking things out, to make sure I am safe.
    While Caesar is saying, 'Count everybody',
        you are looking at me and saying,
        'Everybody counts'.

271   It's all right, Lord, I'll let myself out.
    Day by day I say this,
        longing to be released
        from a life that is no life,
        from a life that has become
        seeming death and absolute pain.
    And yet I carry on, Lord.
    Linger here for a moment only.
    This moment is enough.
    And if I can bear this moment,
        I look no further.

272   Dear Lord, you are my God.
    Early will I seek you.
    My soul waits on you,
        to do your work in me today.
    I bless you in the morning.

Is there a life before death, Lord?   273
That's what I am worried about.
The next world can wait till I get there.
One world at a time,
   one day at a time.
And yes, I know there will be a better tomorrow.
Nothing good can ever be lost.
But I'd like to have the comfort of this morrow,
   around me today.

Lord, I offer you my sins.   274
Anyone can be a success,
   it depends what you are successful at.
But it takes real skill to be a failure.
Absolute skill to be a disaster.
But you managed it,
   in that one moment of time,
   utter dereliction,
   no comfort from man or God at all.
You said, 'It is finished. It is complete.'
You touched me,
   in my own dereliction.

If I go up to heaven, you are there.   275
If I go down to hell, depression's darkest pit,
   you are there also.
You never leave me.
   You sustain me.
And if you cannot rescue,
   you always love me.
Your arms around me for eternity.

276   Keep me away from the pit, Lord.
One more day eked out of life's prison sentence,
    so many years to do,
      when even a fortnight would be enough.
Though it may become also
    a chance to meet you,
    to know you,
    and to share at the end
    my sense of nothingness,
    my loss of identity.

277   It is hard to love you, Lord,
    hard to be certain of your presence.
Yet you are with me, you love me.
And, if I am uncertain of my own response,
    I know my uncertainty is your gift also.
As in the gospel, so now,
    you stand at my door and knock.

278   You know the secrets of my heart.
    You know that I love you.
Deep down beneath my sins
    and ingrained habits of wrong and failure,
    you see the true me.
You love me. You are my friend.

The sea is so large, Lord.   *279*
My boat is so small.
I set out, with the deeps beneath me,
    and the far horizon farther
    than I can travel to,
    or even imagine.
And yet, as well as I may, I am coming.
Using the winds given,
    even though they are all against me,
    and all I can do is veer sideways,
    nearer your kingdom, my destination.

I do not cry to you out of the pit.   *280*
I do not raise my voice.
There is no need.
No need to shout,
    only to whisper quietly in my heart,
    that I need you.
And find you,
    here in the muddy clay,
    beside me.

Help me to close that door.   *281*
It hangs open, swinging on its hinges.
I did not go that way,
    take that path, that job, that preferment,
    that wife or husband.
Help me to live in the now, Lord,
    not in the might-have-been.
Help me to live in the present now.

282   The saddest words in Shakespeare are 'Othello's occupation gone'. And the saddest words in Jesus' parables may have been those of the labourers waiting in the marketplace: 'No one has hired us.'

Jesus always hires us and has work for us to do. Even when that work is only trying to be ourselves.

He found Peter and Andrew fishermen, and turned them into prophets. He found Matthew a tax collector, and gave him employment in another currency. So he finds us today and asks if we will serve him. Even if we cannot do much, and are a 'patient', having things done to us, instead of doing them ourselves.

We are always irreplaceable to God, and serve him even when we do (or seem to do) nothing. Jesus loves us when we are in pyjamas.

283   I find this day a burden,
      this moment a burden.
And yet it is, no doubt, your gift also to me.
A thing given,
      though you yourself only want
      to give me life, not death.
The depression, the darkness
      is a thing you do not wish for me,
      but somehow have to allow.
Help me to remember, Lord,
      the state of the world is not my fault.
The state of my own world,
      so isolated and restricting,
      is even less my fault.
You love me in this disability,
      this slow awkwardness.
You are with me in it, underneath me,
      not above me offering exhortations.
Lord, if I can bear it,
      I'll get out of bed.

Help me to get out of bed, Lord.   *284*
   It is such a long way to the ground.
Astronauts land on the moon,
   but I have this difficult task
   of re-entry into this world's atmosphere
My world's atmosphere.
My own world,
   so alienated, so alone,
   and only I know
   what it is like to be me.
Yet you know me, Lord.
You love me.
You give me my name,
   day by day, hour by hour.
You name the parts of your rifle, each morning.
The parts of your church,
   your kingdom.
It's a long way to the ground, Lord.
   Help me.

Have you a miracle left over, Lord?   *285*
Me, for whom every day is a miracle,
   if I can endure it,
   if you can endure it, in me.
Bring me through it.
Keep me company, in your own apparent absence.
Lord, save me.
Lord, save the world.
Begin with me, Lord,
   in your own unhurried time,
   at my pace.
Not the world's.

286   One day at a time, Lord,
      has always been your policy.
    One hour at a time, this moment now.
    Evensong seems a long way off.
    Supper is a distant Matterhorn
      waiting to be climbed.
    But this moment, Lord,
      holds all my past memories and friends.
    By breathing in now, I love them, am with them.
    In breathing out, I offer you my love.

287   Teatime, Lord.
    I never thought I would get this far,
      but I have, or rather you have.
    And so, by your grace,
      I give you glory
      by being here, not by doing.
    Like Alfred J. Prufrock,
      I measure out my life in coffee spoons.
    Each one such an achievement.
    A candle burning on the poor altar
      of my love for you.

288   It's a nice day, everyone says.
    The sun is shining.
    And yet it's not a nice day in my head.
    Anything but.
    Deep cloud banks of depression,
      constant dark.
    And yet at least, Lord,
      in you I have one person
      who does not say, 'Be sunny'.
    You are sunny,
      only in your kindness toward me,
      this disposition, this constant attitude.

You love me.
In tight cloud banks of grey,
   you pray for water to collect and break.

Lord, please tell me who I am.   *289*
I have changed job,
   been divorced,
   lost my house,
   lost any sense of identity or direction.
Yet you tell me who I am.
Only love can reach certain conditions:
   only you on the cross.
Love is the answer.
What was the question?

Coming aboard

Life is hard enough, without being told we should   *290*
enjoy it. And Jesus did not spend his life telling the
crowds to 'have faith'. He spent his life among people,
trying to give it to them. 'Not menus but food' was
always his response to our needs. As it is today. He
stands before us with his two hands and five fingers on each. Two fishes and five small loaves, all any
of us are issued with for life's picnic. And Jesus says
to us, somehow, hesitantly, not proudly, 'It is enough.'
The five loaves and two small fish: the inadequate
things or circumstances of our own life are somehow enough to feed the world.

   None of us knows the value of our own life.
Especially when we seem to do nothing. 'Whoever
saves (or feeds) one soul, it is as if he had fed the
whole world.'

291 The chess board of my life
   is complicated, Lord.
  Hemmed in on every side,
   in check perpetually,
   by those stronger pieces
   I can never match or remove.
  And yet, Lord,
   weak positions have their grace also.
  Weak pieces, moved by your hand,
   can advance the kingdom
   in ways no one can foresee.

292 You give me faith, Lord,
   not in myself,
   but in my weakness.
  The inabilities of my life
   are places you can visit.
  The empty pages,
   places where you can write.
  Morning by morning you waken me,
   and touch my ear.
  That I may speak to those who are weary,
   a word in season.

293 Release me for service, Lord.
  These chains of my own life
   (no doubt I fastened them)
   which hold me fixed to this limitation,
   this circumstance.
  I am married to my inabilities, Lord.
   What would I do without them?

Help me to remember, Lord,
  as the chains thicken,
  that I am your ambassador in chains.
Yes, I do wish I was a roving ambassador.
But in my cell, you come to me.

Give me back my future, Lord.   294
Or, if that is a diminishing asset,
  give me back my past.
But when that fades also, Lord,
  becoming blurred, inaccessible,
  give me, I ask you, this moment only.

The cross, Lord,   295
  is your ultimate status symbol.
Not the resurrection.
But this inability on your part,
  this failure to move,
  is that which conditions me to your love.
Inability on your part,
  ability on mine,
  to see at last what you are in the world.

Give me faith, Lord.   296
Not in you, but in myself.
Your life in mine.
Give me hope,
  not that you will act well,

you have no option,
but that I will.
Give me love, not for you, Lord.
You have enough already.
But give me love, just a little,
for my own poverty.
Help me to say, 'Well done.'

297   Do you remember
the burning bush, Lord?
Other people saw
a mass of disfigured branches,
dried leaves in need of water.
As I am, dying of neglect,
in apparent plenty.
Starved of love,
though surrounded by people.
But you see the sunlight
through the branches.
You see light in my life,
possibility, shining.
You take off your shoes, Lord,
and enter my life humbly.
To others a sinner,
to you I am your friend.

298   It does not matter if I don't believe in you, Lord.
You believe in me.
It does not matter if I have no sense of your presence.
You have sense of mine. Are mine.
Breath as I breathe.
Feet as I walk.
Closer than my heart, you love me,
and are my friend.

Jesus was known as the friend of publicans and   299
sinners, and was put to death, as love always is, by the
'system' or establishment. He died without any
human consolation, apart from the prayers of two
or three friends. He had no religious consolation. No
sense of triumph for himself in any afterlife, though he
gave comfort as best he could to the two patients in the
beds either side of him, in life's emergency ward. Only
one of them listened. And Jesus' cry of dereliction still
haunts us: 'My God, my God, why have you forsaken
me?' And yet this 'at-one-ment' is seen later as the
moment our human condition touched solid ground.
Ultimate reality: or perhaps un-reality. The state of
not being, of not being able to believe anything.

Should we experience this, may God bless us.
Not in the heavens above, but in our own broken
heart and mind. This is God's dwelling place and
home. 'If I go down to hell, God is there also.'

Help me to forgive myself, Lord,   *300*
    as well as other people.
Help me to know the sun is put there
    to shine on me,
        the rain to wash and refresh.
You don't keep an eye on me, Lord.
You keep both your eyes
    and all your heart, on me, around me.
You are greater than my heart.
You know all things.
When I hold up my hands
    and say, 'It's my fault, I am to blame',
you thank me, but also add,
    'Don't take all the blame, child,
    I need some of it myself.'
And underneath are the everlasting arms
    that this falling, falling, falling
    can't fall through.

301   Help me to be easy with myself, Lord,
        patient, kind.
I am not a wheelbarrow, needing to be pushed.
But a child, needing to be loved,
    coaxed into virtue.
Help me to appreciate the flowers in my garden.
They won't grow any quicker
    by being criticised.
They need the constant rain and warm sunshine
    of your love, your approval.
Shine on me, Lord.
It's your job to do so.

302   Thank you for not telling me to cheer up, Lord.
The world is hard enough
    without having to enjoy ourselves.
Thank you for not telling me 'not to worry';
I tried once not to worry, but failed.
I ended up worrying because I couldn't stop worrying.
But you break these ever-decreasing circles,
    break the endless cycle of guilt
    engendering effort,
    engendering failure,
    engendering more guilt.
Put simply, you love me.

303   I have an eye on the clock, Lord.
But two feet on the ground are better.
Help me to do those earthly things
    that bring me blessing.
Take whatever blessings life offers.

Life passes away, Lord,
  as I read these words,
  live this moment.
Help me, quietly,
  return it to you.

Help me to look at the sun, Lord.   *304*
I, who do not feel the warmth of the sun,
  hope it shines on others.
In the darkness you love me, Lord.
Come to me, across the waters
  of my own failures.
In the sunshine, though I do not feel your warmth,
  you share my dereliction.

I sing of what I want to believe, Lord,   *305*
  or would do, if I had better voice,
  and better heart.
Help me to remember as I go about my tasks;
  not too many,
  for then I'd get tired;
  not too few,
  for then my mind would over-race my body.
Help me to remember this only in the darkness:
  you believe in me.

306   Are you there, Lord?
If so, you're keeping remarkably quiet.
Can you not come to me in this breakdown,
    when I have no sense of your presence
    and maybe, never have.
Help me to remember, Lord,
    you are with me when I don't feel you.
Especially then
    your own experience of the human condition
    speaks to me.
Forsaken. But why?
No comfort at all,
    the tree devoid utterly of any leaves,
    except this bare truth that you love me
    in my nakedness,
    all virtues or social occasions stripped away.
You love me to the end.

307   Thank you for taking my 'breakdown'
    seriously, Lord,
    but for laughing also
    at things we can laugh at together.
Thank you for loving me,
    not trying to hurry me,
    not trying to make me 'normal',
    crank me up.
Thank you for seeing me behind my condition.
You take my illness seriously,
    but me more seriously still.

Listen to what I say, Lord.   *308*
Not what I am.
Do what I ask, Lord.
My requests are always better than my life.
My alleluias sound well,
   my life sounds ill at ease,
   and out of tune.
But you love your sparrows, Lord,
   your crows as well as your nightingales.
And knowing this,
   I praise you in the morning.

Thank you for coming to my funeral, Lord.   *309*
Not the hymns and eulogies,
   the prayers and pauses,
   the coffin's slow carrying in and out.
But thank you for coming to me,
   receiving me, lifting me up.
Thank you for coming
   to my resurrection.

Thank you for my insecurity, Lord.   *310*
Where would I be without it?
I should be insufferable in my success,
   and list of things achieved.
But I have only one achievement, Lord,
   of knowing that you love me.
And this one person I shall meet today.
Whoever blesses one person,
   it is as if he has blessed the whole world.
I'm ready to bless the world, Lord,
   with this weakness.

311   Some people are eagles, Lord.
Able to fly at the sun direct.
See their ways.
Feel their purposes.
But I am one of your sparrows, Lord.
The smallest coins in human currency.
Sold for a farthing.
Two small doves,
    the price your servants paid for Jesus' birth.
Eight days old at the temple,
    another Jew, another poor citizen.
And yet I am not poor, Lord,
    caged, waiting to be offered.
Free in my own limited way,
    I stretch out my wings, and fly.

312   Help me to take the tablets, Lord.
Not to let me out finally,
    but help me to endure
    one day,
    one moment
    at a time.

313   Those who follow Jesus in darkness do a great work. The wise men followed the star to Bethlehem, which comforted them. But they went home in darkness, by an unfamiliar route, that Jesus might live and grow in safety.

    We who follow Jesus in darkness also help him to live, in others.

Is this what they call the 'dark night of the soul'?   *314*
In that case, Lord, I'd have preferred the early evening.
I understand now why five thousand
   turned up to your picnic
   but only three to your crucifixion.
You got it wrong, Lord,
   or perhaps we did.
Perhaps the five loaves and two small fish
   were on Good Friday also
   your chief congregation.
Two or three at the cross's foot,
   a small congregation.
All I may see today
   in my bed-sittingroom of a life.
But you are there with us,
   helping us to feed a whole world.

Don't take my mind to bits, Lord,   *315*
   it's been dismantled enough already.
Taxed beyond endurance,
   its parts strained and broken,
   its fuses blown.
But you loved me, Lord,
   when I was a baby and could do nothing.
You'll love me when I'm old and senile,
   if I get so far, and can do nothing again.
I don't need to justify myself to you, Lord.
   You are in me already, doing just that.
But give me one simple task, Lord,
   one simpleness of visit or letter I can do.
May I find rest and re-creation in that.

316 When I am weak, Lord,
   then I am strong.
 When I have nothing left,
  except this present
  moment of weakness,
  you come to me, bless me,
  are well satisfied with your creation,
  and still say,
  'I have done all things well.'

317 Water is a good thing to walk on, Lord,
   though it leaves no apparent footprints.
 Dry land is so much harder.
 These fluid situations,
  these fragile circumstances
  that will bear no weight at all,
  except love's weight
  which is no burden.
 Come to me,
  walking over the water.
 Those situations that will not bear examination
  only bring me closer to you.

318 We have no record, Lord,
  of how much you did,
  how often you got into Peter's boat,
  how loudly you spoke.
 Only how you lived, this one thing you said,
  that you loved me well,
  and made all things,
  your life especially,
  for my sake.

You are greater than my heart, Lord.   *319*
You know all things.
You forgive all things.
You bear all things.
You keep no score of wrongs,
    only of my attempts or wishes
    to serve you better,
    know you,
    love you,
    walk beside you in the darkness.
Shine, Lord, where you can.

Don't be hard on yourself, son.   *320*
Don't judge yourself so harshly, daughter.
God is your father and mother rolled into one.
He is the one who dies for you daily.
He looks beneath your sins,
    to see his son, his daughter.
He sees what you are now,
    and shall be later, in eternity.

Out of the deep have I called to you.   *321*
Out of the tomb, out of the sepulchre.
Bandages wrapped round, securing me firmly.
No chance of escape,
    but you call me through the bandages.
I cannot alter life's complications.
You call me through the grave-clothes,
    and one day will roll back the stone.

322   I cling to the wreckage, Lord,
       though I would rather be sitting in the boat,
       steering it, helping you to.
    But perhaps I am in the boat, Lord.
    Your family, your boat,
       so frail in its human condition.
    Peter and Andrew, pray for me.
    James and John, lower your nets.
    I'm not coming aboard,
       but am with you already.

323   It's all a pretence, Lord,
       these prayers I say,
       this attitude I put on.
    I don't feel it,
       do not feel anything,
       only emptiness,
       the dark side of the soul.
    But one day I shall by your grace,
       and my patience, wake up
       after your likeness.
    And be
       well satisfied.

Deep waters

324   The story of Jesus' life is that all of us have our unique meaning. If we are born in a stable, unable to find accommodation, God will send shepherds to watch over us. If of uncertain parentage, God himself and Joseph will be our father. Sending wise men from the distant corners of the earth, to show that our one solitary life will still bless and influence the world.

And if we die forsaken on a cross, with no human or religious consolation, there is one at least who sends angels to open up our grave, bringing us out of our grave-clothes, and saying, 'Our living has not been in vain'.

As we get older we are like John the fisherman, the only disciple to grow old and lose his memory. He stretched out his arms to old age, and found himself bound with cords he did not wish, and taken to situations he never expected. In old age also, though we cannot sense it, God loves us and is our friend.

Do I exist, Lord?   *325*
I am sure you do.
And because you exist, I exist also.
You are always thinking of me,
    always loving me.
Yet I wonder often,
    my mind eroded away
    by the world's neglect,
    no one saying thank you,
    no one acknowledging
    my attempts to contribute.
I wonder how you feel, Lord.
Much the same, I wouldn't wonder!

When my mother and father leave me,   *326*
    your love holds me up.
When my children grow up and leave home,
    your love protects them wherever they go.
Your love protects me also,
    surrounds me, enables me.
Lord, you are always with me.
Till the world's end, and beyond.

327   Get a move on, Lord.
No one else will.
Let your trumpets sound, for a change.
Let the walls of apathy and neglect
    come tumbling down.
I've walked about the city long enough.
So have you, I imagine.
The trumpets are all ready in your hand.
One, two, three . . .
    the countdown to your kingdom has begun!

328   Help me to seek your glory, Lord,
    but also my own.
My own place in your kingdom
    no one else can fill.
My own calling, down by Galilee's shore,
    where I first met you, among the lobster pots.
Swiftly you come to my aid,
    now, as you did then.
You see me under the fig tree,
    in the shadow of my own home.
You call to me.
Your voice gives me meaning.

329   I thank you, Lord,
    for all the blessings of my life.
Those souls I have been able to help.
Those who have loved me.
Those good things I was able to try,
    even if they did not turn out

as I had planned,
  you had envisaged.
I fill my mind with your love, Lord.
In all weathers you come to me,
  and are my friend.

Take me out of the pit, dear Lord.   330
For your glory, not mine.
Raise me up,
  bind your love around me,
  uphold me, save me.
And if you cannot deliver me, Lord,
  from the pit,
  deliver me in it.
Come to me.
Share my life.
Uphold me.

As the deer longs for the water-brook,   331
  so does my soul long for you.
Even if one leg is broken,
  I come to you.
You wait for me,
  and give me your word.
As the eagle flies to your glory,
  so do I live.
Even if one wing is damaged,
  the currents of your love uphold me,
  bless me.
I rest on your love.
As the fish in the sea,
  I make use of the currents,
  to swim to your glory.

332   Dear Lord, you are my shepherd.
        Emperors count their subjects,
            prime ministers their votes.
        But you only count me your friend.
        Day by day you count me.
        You know me by name.
        Your love calls me, leads me on.
        Your flock is never complete
            till I am inside.
        While the Emperor shouts, 'Count everybody',
            you look at me and say, 'My life is enough'.

333   I look at the stars, Lord,
            all the heavens and galaxies
            your love has created.
        I feel so small beneath them,
            yet you have made them, for my sake.
        I count the stars,
            stretching away beyond infinity.
        But you count the possibilities of my life.
        Your spirit comes to me.
        In all the stars in love's firmament,
            I have my special place,
            and shine to your glory.

334   Can a bad gardener be a good priest, Lord?
        I don't know.
        Only that you nourish my soul,
            and tend each plant in my garden.
        Who knows to what size
            the smallest plant may grow?

Was it a case of mistaken identity, Lord?   335
We who took you for the gardener,
    up so early on the first day
    of the world's week,
    planting new seeds in our flower bed,
    so glad to see us,
    encouraging every sign of life,
    however small above the soil.
It is a new world again today, Lord,
    a new Eden.
And so, I do not think it was a case of mistaken identity,
    but of identity taken, and used
    to bless our souls for ever.

I serve you in fear, Lord.   336
Not in fear of you hurting me,
    but of me hurting you.
I set out on your journey.
I climb your mountain.
I respect the heights and depths this life has to offer.
Use the ropes and tackle available.
Breathing your air,
    I fill my lungs with your goodness.
I approach the summit.

We all say 'Amen', Lord,   337
    in our own way.
Each of us has our own place
    in that galaxy of human souls
    that shine to your glory.
I shine to your glory, Lord,

not with my own light,
but in my own way.
This day
I give you glory.

338   Dear Lord,
       you are my rock.
I build my house on you,
       this day on you.
With the materials you have given me.
Who am I to say,
       who is anyone to say,
       the materials you have given me
       are inadequate?
And if they are inadequate,
       that is only to stop me building
       taller houses than my neighbours'.
The weaker the material,
       the closer I will build to the ground.

339   It's not where I am now, Lord,
       that defines me,
       but where I am looking.
Not what I have now,
       but what I will have,
       what will possess me,
       in the future.
Lord, my eyes are fixed on you
       and on your kingdom,
as your eyes are fixed,
       and your heart is fixed,
       on my welfare for ever.

Show me your spirit, Lord.   340
Let your star shine again.
Leading us forward
    through the dark places
    to our journey's end.
The end of this day.

My bags are packed, Lord,   341
    I am ready to leave.
I have sent on many of my attributes,
    except that one attribute
    you yourself have given me.
The less I have here on earth,
    the more there is waiting for me
    on the other side.
More friends, more mountains to climb,
    more paths to explore.
Meanwhile I cherish this last gift,
    and also the first you gave me.
I am always myself,
    and you give me meaning.

I am tired of being told, Lord,   342
    to lift up my heart.
I want somewhere to put it down.
Foxes have holes,
    birds have nests,
    but we have nowhere
    to lay our heads,
    or our hearts,
    except in you, who travel with us.

343   You are Lord of my health, not of my sickness.
Yet you are Lord in my sickness.
Leading my soul by your still waters.
Feeding me, feeding my imagination.
Whatever things are of good report,
   helpful to me.
Whatever things are clean, lovely and helpful,
   clean, lovely and helpful to me,
I think on these things.
And lay my soul down to rest,
   by your river.

344   I set my troubled heart at rest,
   in your word, but also your silences.
Day by day I rest my soul
   in your refusal to judge me,
   refusal to leave me,
   refusal to write me off.
To you I am never redundant.
Always essential, to your plans,
   to the world's blessing.

345   I long for a big service, Lord. As Elijah did.
Clergy, choirs, robes,
   the movement of vestments to solemn music.
But all you gave him is all you give us.
A broken heart.
A life that wished it had done better.
An altar soaked in tears.
By your love
   it still shall catch fire.
'A broken and a contrite heart,
   you will not despise.'

Help me to remember the use of silence, Lord,   *346*
   my silence, not other people's.
Help me to pray for my friends, Lord.
I meet them today.
They will make their journey
   to my life in their own time.
Help me to remember them
   when they have gone.
That will make their journey home safer.
Help me to be available to your needs in them.
Now and always.

I tend to expect the worst, Lord.   *347*
Usually I am right!
And if things do go well,
   I cannot feel it.
But you can.
You know the value of my life.
Lift me up, then, in your love.
Let me forget all things,
   except your love for me,
   this tenderness.
Wrap your arms around me,
   clothe me in your love,
   and let my own mind be restored,
   in all these moments you have given me.

Dear Lord, I praise you.   *348*
My praise is precious to you.
My life matters.
Like the two sparrows sold for a farthing,
   my cries are heard

along with all the praises
of the great congregations.
My prayers rise up to you,
you listen to me,
and hear me gladly,
and in my heart and voice,
help me to pray.

349   Help us to look beyond the prayer book, Lord.
Beyond the prayers,
beyond the hymns,
to you who are the source of our life.
Help us to praise you in the morning.

350   Do you have a celibacy guidance bureau, Lord,
for those who have difficulty,
living with themselves?
I go to bed, and I am there.
Still there in the morning,
and on the farthest business-trip,
all airports are the same, and so am I.
And yet, I am not the same to you.
Day by day the light casts new shadows
and nuances of love
on my life.
Things not seen before, are noticed afresh by you.

351   Behold what manner of love
the Father has shown us.
For you call us friends, Lord,
not patients, cases, candidates.
And yet we are candidates for your love.

Suitable cases for your treatment,
   of unbridled affection.
And yes, we are patient also,
   as we listen to your word,
   morning by morning.

In your law will I exercise myself, Lord.   *352*
Gentle press-ups, and knees-bending,
   in the art of your love.
You who ask for our friendship,
   not our success.
Our attempts at constancy,
   never our achievement.
You who love us, world without end,
   and beyond the world's end,
   without judgement.

Do you remember the phone, Lord?   *353*
It used to be an intrusion.
As I was going out,
   or staying in,
   working at that canvas
   you yourself had provided
   for that day.
But now it is silent
   and I have time to pray,
   thinking of one person a day,
   before I phone.
Two minutes on my knees.
Twenty seconds.
Whoever does not begin
   by kneeling down
   runs every possible risk.

354   The night is your territory also, Lord.
You are king in the dark hours also,
   though my soul does not see it.
You are my shepherd,
   watching over me in the darkness.
You know me by name.
You love me.
You call me to your service.
You call me your friend.

355   Lord, you are the first person I talk to.
Before I talk to you,
   listen to your silences,
   I am in no state to talk with anyone else,
   or listen to you in them,
   your word in them.

356   Help me not to dwell on the past, Lord.
I was happier then.
Or if not happier, had hopes of happiness,
   knew where I was,
   had some sense of my own identity,
   my place in the world,
   your plans for me.
No doubt I could never approach them.
Who can? But I had some sense of 'belonging'.
But now I look back on these snapshots,
   people who were young when I was young,
   and have now arrived in the world,
   while I am lost,
   peering out from their daughters' weddings,
   members of the golf club,

members of that human family
from which I am barred.
Your spirit blesses them, Lord, through me.
You lift me up.
My childhood is safe somewhere.
You help me to unlatch my own blinds.
The light coming in is dull,
    but part of a greater light
    shining on me, in your love.

I have no need to shout, Lord.   357
The quietest whisper is enough.
The sound of our need
    is your opportunity.
The brokenness of our heart
    the only music needed.

I would have asked you   358
    back to earth, Lord,
    but my mind was somehow occupied
    with other things.
The children's schooling,
    my own career,
    my family's prospects.
And yet we have no better prospect, Lord,
    than that of your return.
No better schooling
    than the learning of your love.
No better career
    than that of serving you.
In all of these things, Lord,
    you return daily.

359   I bear the burden
          and heat of the day, Lord.
    Your burden. Your day. Your heat.
    I'd rather have a cheerful breeze
          down from the seven hills
          that surround your city.
    I understand that breezes are not made to order,
          blown to order.
    They blow as they will;
          yet so does your good spirit,
          comforting me, refreshing me.

360   Why is it, Lord, that incurable diseases
          are so much easier to heal,
          than those of the mildly indisposed?
    Is it because my desperation
          opens a door to your kingdom
          others cannot find?
    My life holds a key that turns the lock
          in a way never turned before?
    Come then, Lord.
    You who are my door and home.

361   The main feature of Jesus' life was not that he healed more people than anyone else. Though his disciples, who had so misunderstood his ministry at the time, liked to think, looking back, that he had. In fact he healed those who needed him, as he was able, or the Father was able, in the one needing help. No doubt, in this way, the few 'miracles' of love were like the loaves and fishes, to influence the world. But the main feature of Jesus' healing was not the number healed, or the few who remained with him to say 'thank you' or be 'evidence'. The main and only feature of Jesus' ministry was his love.

It's all a trick, Lord.   *362*
I'll never get out of this world alive.
But you managed it.
In one moment
   of pure affection
   for my sake,
   you shouted 'It is finished.'
So it is, Lord.
I am your work now.
Your responsibility,
   as you are mine.

I've had this illness   *363*
   twelve years, Lord.
For ages, then.
I can't remember how long.
All right then,
   this illness has had me.
But though it has trapped me,
   it has never defined me.
I am your child,
   held by temporary chains.
The chains loosen,
   they are tired of seeming in control,
   but always knowing
   you are in control, Lord.
You the unchained one,
   who loosens my bonds.
You the chained one,
   who sings alleluia.

364   Familiarity breeds contempt. Sometimes it can also breed attempt, and the chance to follow Jesus more easily (more comfortably or securely), though life is never easy or comfortable.

Peter's fishing boat is also ours, with its place for Jesus' head to rest in the storm, and Andrew's lobster pots, and the smell of varnish. Familiar things and prayers can help us as we grow older. Most of us come into the world hoping to be doctors, but end up being patients. As Jesus did, when he died in life's emergency ward, with two thieves or bandits in the beds on either side of him. Even then, though his arms were stretched out, and life had taken him where he had no wish to go, he found opportunity to bless others.

365   My life seems to be a history of mistakes,
        as all lives are.
Being human is a messy business, Lord,
        and your first disciples weren't saints,
        till they were dead.
In their lifetime they were messy saints.
You had to wash the smell of seaweed
        out of their sandals.
Lord, help me to turn my sins to your glory.
One day I will be sinless and smiling,
        and possibly no use to anybody!
No one can stand a successful smiler!
But a failure, Lord, evokes sympathy.
His expressions for others' welfare
        enter the heart closely.
So Lord, I thank you in my sins,
        as you love me,

one by one,
my sins are blessed by,
received by,
taken by,
your love.

Help me to say goodbye to the past, Lord.   *366*
God be with you.
Rest in peace.
The past is in your hands, Lord.
It is never wasted.
Mistakes and virtues alike
    mingle beneath the soil,
    subside, in your own time, and theirs,
    plants will grow.
Others will tend them,
    others pick your fruit.
Help me to say goodbye to the past, Lord.
    It is alive in you.

Saying goodbye to the past is a great matter and so   *367*
many people never manage it. Lot's wife kept looking
to the past and saying, 'Things were not done like
this in my grandfather's day.' She became fixed, like
a block of salt, or a record stuck in its groove.

The children of Israel also looked to the past.
But it was memories pressed together to become
solid ground, on which to build present lives. Not
a sofa but a springboard. So may our memories be.

368 You use parts of my soul
   I never knew existed, Lord.
  Muscles I never knew I had
   have been exercised in my life
   by Galilee's beach.
  But you took my boat
   from Galilee, Lord,
   out into the world,
   to catch your fish there,
   feed your people there.
  Looking over the edge of my boat
   into your deep waters,
   I was conscious of my own littleness,
   but of your love, above all.

369 The kingdom of heaven,
   your kingdom, Lord,
   is for the desperate,
   not the well-meaning.
  It is for us,
   desperate for your return,
   desperate in our own weakness,
   that makes us rely on your strength,
   your grace only.
  Your love comes to us quickly,
   comes to us daily.

370 Help me to build your castle, Lord,
   not in the air, but on the ground.
  From the floor up.
  Foundations first.

Walls in place.
Girders.
Cement to be mixed.
Here on the ground, Lord,
   beside your crib,
   I give you glory.

And would it have been the same, Lord,   *371*
   if you had retired to Tunbridge Wells
   and grown roses?
Rejected by society,
   your Church closing her doors,
   until your health collapsed,
   your mind broke,
   and nobody cared.
But we cared, Lord.
In your nursing home we came to you.
Listened to your broken mind reciting Galilee.
We bound you up.
Rolled aside the stone from your life's sepulchre,
   and proclaimed you are alive.

Help me to rest in your word, Lord.   *372*
There is no need always to be speaking it.
Help me to rest in your love.
There is no need always to be showing it.
Help me to rest in you,
   for if I do that, in your own time and my own,
your word and your love will percolate outward.

For sinners only

373   Jesus' religion, if he had one, was a religion for sinners. Peter and Paul were the chief exponents because they made most mistakes. 'Pray for all sinners of whom I am the chief' (Paul). Or, in Arabic terms, weave your mistakes into the fabric of your life. Do not always feel you have to unpick the threads. All lives are histories of errors and sins and missed opportunities, made opportune.

374   I'm not always as happy as I look, Lord.
My mouth smiles, but my heart doesn't.
My heart is in pain, in darkness,
   while my mouth broadcasts kind messages,
   messages of hope I do not feel.
But you love me, Lord.
You love to see me smile
   but love me in my anguish even more.
You are not a fair-weather friend,
   but a friend in all weathers.
When the shutters are down,
   and the wind blows, you come to me,
   and make my soul your home.

375   I see the dark side of your face, Lord.
I feel the dark side, love's absence,
   lack of purpose in my own life.
But you are my purpose, Lord,
   and my song.
You are also my memory,
   my strength, my future.
Help me to hold your hand, Lord.
   Even when I can't feel it.

What do you mean,
    I'm not doing anything, Lord?
I'm worrying!
Is not that enough?
To feel the pains of the world,
    before the world itself notices them.
To feel my children's dangers,
    while they walk carefree.
One day, Lord, I shall walk
    carefree in your presence.
But till then I love you in darkness,
    and thank you for worrying about me.

376

We have the power to hurt, Lord.
You have only the power to be hurt.
Help me when I grow old, Lord.
I am older today than yesterday.
Help me to see my helplessness
    as your opportunity.
My weakness as your strength.

377

We don't always get to die when we expect, Lord.
A slow graceful exit,
    the world seeing, you seeing
    what we have done.
But in the world's time
    we are broken and brought low,
    made ill and poor
    when we can ill afford lt.
Our only comfort
    is that you, in darkness,
    are outside the camp also.

378

379   Help me to remember, Lord,
        death is not a failure to be alive.
    Sickness is not a failure to be well.
    This day we endure.
    No, I am not my own master.
    This condition I accept;
        no, I did not will it,
        and can only move forward
        at a snail's pace.
    To be stationary, sometimes,
        is a great advancement.

380   Each life has its own meaning, Lord,
        though we often do not see it at the time.
    Only at the end, journey completed,
        will I look back on my false steps,
        twisting footprints and see,
        even in the darkest times,
        how you were leading me,
        carrying me, walking beside me.

381   We don't always get the illnesses we choose, Lord.
    Sometimes they choose us.
    Coming on us suddenly, unawares.
    This one condition we were not prepared for,
        helplessness, inability to choose another way.
    Lord, I hold out my hands to you in helplessness,
        I cannot serve you now, only love you.
    Yet this attention to your word
      is all you ever need
        to save the world through my weakness.

Give me a prayer book, Lord,   *382*
    that will help me last till supper.
However poor its pages,
    they will be well thumbed.
Till the prayer of need and emptiness
    and not being, not experiencing,
    is taken up into your darkness.
You live there, Lord, giving light to others,
    but have no sense of it yourself.
Star shining for me,
    star shining in me,
    but not noticing,
    never conscious of,
    its own painful progress.

Help me, Lord, to use   *383*
    the life that I am given,
    in your way, my way,
    and no one else's.
The cards I am dealt
    no doubt could be better,
    but they provide,
    even the lower ones,
    some chance of contributing
    to the world's game.
Only you know the score, Lord.
Only you know who is winning,
    and at what.

384   Help me to make the most of my life, Lord.
The most of my death.
This slow undressing of my powers.
Each life having a beginning, middle and end.
But only you know which order they come in.
Which is my true 'end',
    my life's work,
      that soul for which I was created.
Those lives for which I was put down
    on earth's entry list.
So many years of tenure in another's property,
    until at last you call me home.

385   Some stones, Lord, cannot be moved.
Their massive solidity defies us.
We cannot turn them to bread.
Only live in their shadow.
Walk around them,
    build our lives on our own failures,
    our own nothingness.
But you, Lord, who see we have nothing,
    love us,
    remember how it was at our beginning.
Helpless then, helpless now,
    the world is still my cradle.

386   Help me to practise the faith, Lord.
I can't be expected to get the hang of it,
    get the hang of your love for me,
    which defies logic,
    and yet has its own crazy inner constancy.
That you love me always.
However I look,
    whatever I do,
    however I feel.

Help me to grasp the point of your life, Lord.   *387*
Its point being that it has no point.
Your agenda being that you have no agenda,
   beyond the agenda of my own life,
    my own happiness.
Dear Lord, work out your agenda in me.

Books about water, Lord, I don't need,   *388*
   I who am a fish in your sea.
Books about air are no help,
   to one who wishes only to fly in your sky.
Help me to fly, Lord,
   resting on your love.
Help me swim in
   that ocean of your affection I can never see.
Hold it, Lord,
   I'm coming.
As well as I can.
One awkward step at a time.

Thank you, Lord, for knowing me   *389*
   better than I know myself.
For loving me,
   more than I love myself.
For forgiving me,
   more than I ever can begin to.
Thank you for believing in me,
   long after I gave up hope.
For seeing my future,
   when I saw only darkness.
Thank you for being beyond the darkness,
   in the darkness, my friend.

'Sinners only need apply'

390   I saw the notice, Lord,
      on your first church.
Built of wood and straw,
      in Bethlehem.
The ox and ass,
      your first congregation,
      thinking to themselves
      what good taste you showed
      in calling them.
And so you call me to another day.

391   Dear Lord,
      I am one of those people
      on the wrong side of life's road,
      as the people pass me by
      on the way to Jericho,
      on their way from the holy city.
I try to make the journey
      but find it too much for me.
Half dead and half alive,
      I am only able to listen now and wait,
      as well as I may,
      for the sound of your donkey's footsteps.
Please stop, Lord,
      as I know you always do.
Stop, pick me up,
      carry me to safety.
It is your journey, Lord;
      you make it with me.

Dear Lord, you know that the territorial instinct 392
   is for us humans the most basic instinct of all.
But what of us who have no territory,
   and no place to lay our head and call our own?
We are moved on.
We have no chance to develop and grow.
But our roots are in you, Lord;
   the one without territory, without space,
   who yet gives us space to be ourselves,
   and is our territory and home for ever.

Growing older

When we are young, we set out on journeys to the 393
empty tomb on Sunday morning, and get there first.
We outrun Peter, who is older and short of breath.
But when we are old, another in the form of old
age or sickness binds us fast and takes us where we
have no wish to go. We are patients. Things happen
to us. We do not apparently make them happen.

   But in our old age, or vulnerability and helplessness also, God is our friend. He watches over us and
leads us, though we have no sense of his presence.

   John the apostle was the only disciple to know
this. He lived to old age, looked back in love, and
had arthritis.

Is there a life after Galilee, Lord? 394
I know I am getting older.
All right, then, I have got old.
I feel young inside,
   but to others I seem older,
   and they laugh as I retell
   the Galilee experience;

build a theme park of the time
when your catholic Church
could get in a fishing boat.
Help me not to build theme parks, Lord,
    but rest in your spirit,
    carrying Galilee with me,
    the true waves of your love
    washing me clean.

395   Lord, I bless you in my weakness.
As the shadow of my life grows long.
And the list of people I have known,
    places I have visited,
    things I have done,
    is longer than the list of things,
    people, places that are to be.
But I am myself, Lord.
As I was before I did anything,
    went anywhere, met anybody.
I am myself, as I will be at the end.
Simply your servant
    whom you delight in.

396   We all die at different speeds, Lord.
This slow undressing of our powers.
Eyesight, hearing, teeth and hair falling out,
    our memory going.
Have I told you this before?
Or have you only told me one thing,
    all my life long?
I am always your servant,
    in your good employment,
    as the day ends.

All sickness or old age is a 'taking of us where have   *397*
no wish to go'. In old age and breakdown we are
God's friends also, and may do more than we ever
realise. We are always indispensable to God. As we
get older, the past may be the only thing we have
left. It is in any case more secure. The blessings we
have helped others to can never be taken away. The
sins we have committed can only be forgiven.

There is no need to dwell on the past, except
with love. Even if we are old and broken, the future
belongs to us especially, as it does to the young.

Old age is a blessing, not a failure to be young.
Love gathers up the fragments that remain that
nothing be lost.

Youth is glorious, Lord,   *398*
    though it is not a career.
Old age has its honour too, Lord,
    though fewer people see it.
Fewer people, hardly any people,
    come up to my inadequate speech,
    and blurred memory, and uncertain vision,
    to congratulate me,
    to bless me for this weakness,
    as they did, years ago,
    when in my cot
    I was similarly disadvantaged.
But you see my disadvantage
    as your advantage, Lord.
You bless me.
After so many wounds and failures,
    I still cling to you.
Lord, I thank you
    for what you have given me,
    for what you have taken away,
    for what you have left me.

399   I have started counting my Christmas cards, Lord.
How much am I valued?
How much am I worth?
As the cards get less, Lord,
    what used to be a nuisance,
    cluttering up the mantelpiece,
    becomes a triumph.
I count each one lovingly.
Fewer than last year.
I am getting old.
Most of my friends are beside the crib now,
    not talking about it.

400   When I was young, Lord,
    I put my own clothes on, to some extent.
The clothes I was given,
    heredity and my own circumstances provided.
But now I am older, Lord,
    and I stretch out my arms,
    another, in sickness or breakdown,
    takes me where I have no wish to go.
I have no option,
    things happen to me.
I used to make them happen.
In all of this, Lord,
    you walk beside me and smile,
    and say, 'Well done!'
As well as I may
    I struggle to say your favourite word:
    Amen.
There. I've managed it!
May your kingdom come in my weakness now.
So be it.

Each life has a beginning, Lord, 401
  a middle, and an end.
But not necessarily in that order.
Help me to remember then,
  as I approach my closing years,
  enter them, endure them,
  this slow undressing of my powers.
Help me to know this only,
  my end is not necessarily the defining of my life.
My true conclusion may have come earlier,
  and be kept safe for me, as death approaches.
Nothing good, Lord, is ever lost,
  only deferred.

Do not leave us, Lord, 402
  when we are old and grey-headed.
Come to us in your strength,
  though we are weaker.
Come to us in your power.
Make us strong
  in the memory of your kindness.
May our hearts be deep
  because of our sins forgiven
  and friends retained.
Nothing is lost, Lord.
We are safe in your hands for ever.

I am all alone, Lord. 403
My partner has died,
  the children have left home.
And even if they have not,
  they have their own lives to lead,
  their own agendas,

and I, who was once their stay and centre,
am no longer so essential,
except by my prayer, to them.
Help me to remember, Lord,
as my life collapses,
that I am always essential to you.
You can manage the world, without me,
and have done so for some time.
But though you can manage, Lord,
I'm not sure you want to.

404   One difficulty of growing old is that no one else can see it happening. Only we can see ourselves, where inside we remain always fifteen or seventeen or twenty-five. Others can only see the outside, and may be helpful in telling us how well we have already done. And pointing out that our broken mind or memory is only a sign of how much we have already borne, or been asked to remember.

Sometimes inactivity can be a blessing, though usually we need activity of a different sort. In old age or illness we still need to be needed. Our occupation is never gone. Only changed.

405   We praise you in the evening of our lives,
when the nets
we have let down
at your command,
into your sea,
have taken nothing.
We praise you in the desert places,
when we have nothing to eat,
and day is nearly over.

We praise you when the oil
   in our lamp runs low,
   and there is no replacement,
   no refilling.
We praise you in the darkness, Lord,
   and await your morning.

Night

Jesus of Nazareth left us his crucifixion. It was all he   *406* had to leave ultimately. His utter failure to convert the world, which was perhaps, in retrospect, better than other people's success in manipulating it.

But if Jesus only left his cross, Peter and Andrew at least left their fishing boat. Which is where Christians find comfort too. A lot of religious custom is to help people avoid too much crucifixion: too much reality. The smell of the varnish on Peter's boat, the rowlocks and oars in place, and Thomas' fishing net, are all comforts, like the prayers we say, to help us feel at home. That each of us has our own place in the boat. And our own contribution to the journey. It is important then to know where our waste paper basket is. To have places in the boat or on land where we can go to sleep, and not be disturbed. We need all the comfort we can get. Help to bear our own cross, and help with our burdens.

The problem always remains acute. Not whether God exists, but whether we do: and, if so, how?

407   The night comes, Lord,
       when no one can work.
    Help me to remember you, Lord,
       or if I cannot manage that,
       help me to know you do not forget me.
    Those long sleepless nights,
       when I look over the edge of my life,
       and seem to have taken nothing,
       it is all in vain.
    It is not in vain, Lord.
    You come to me in the darkness,
       walking over the water.
    You are on the edge of the shore,
       preparing my breakfast.

408   The night comes, when no one can work.
    Nor should we be expected to.
    The ending of any day, or sport or activity,
       is not failure on my aching limbs' part,
       my aching mind's.
    It is a chance to look back over the day,
       what has gone before,
       and rejoice in blessings given,
       pray for blessings
       in situations left empty.
    No one can do everything, Lord.
    Not even you, all in one go.
    Lord, I bless you in the evening,
       and do not regard it as 'a failed morning'.
    Each hour, each moment,
       has its glory.

Out of the deep,   409
    I call to you, Lord.
The deep anguish of things
    closes me around.
There is no way out.
If there were,
    honourably,
    possibly,
    you would have given it,
    I might have taken it.
But now it seems too late.
Bless my lost opportunities, Lord;
    paths not taken, years ago.
They are not lost opportunities,
    only opportunity deferred.
    A chance for you to love me now.

When I am awake at night,   410
    toiling in my imagination,
    catching nothing,
    you come to me over the water.
What cannot sustain me,
    what cannot sustain anyone,
    is enough to convey your love.

411   Jesus was asleep sometimes when he should have
       been awake. And awake when everyone else was
       resting. In the boat on Lake Galilee, with the waves
       rising higher and the wind roaring against the
       sails, Jesus slept with his head on a cushion. He
       could do nothing about the weather, and his disci-
       ples upbraided him for it. Later in the garden of
       Gethsemane he remained awake to the human
       condition and his own betrayal, which was all he
       had left with which to bless the world and show
       goodwill. His disciples all slept then and were
       concerned he did not do the same.
           May God bless us and help us to sleep, when we
       can do nothing about the weather. May he help us
       to be awake to betrayals no one else can see.

412   Thank you for my sleeplessness, Lord,
               turning over in bed,
               turning over the problems of the day.
       They seem bigger, Lord, they are bigger.
       They weigh me down, but not out.
       I wish I could sleep.
       And yet, Lord, this sleeplessness is your blessing.
       You cannot sleep either,
               for all the sins of the world.
       You lie awake, you stand awake,
               shepherd in my field, watching over me.

413   Help me to remember, Lord,
               you don't will my sufferings,
               though you do in a sense permit them.
        You are the fount of my life,
               but are yourself constantly thwarted
               in your love of me.

You love me,
  but the world is dark.
You come to me,
  but I cannot feel you, cannot see you.
I am like the fish
  who did not believe in water.
Help me, Lord, to swim in your love.

My wife is sleeping soundly, Lord.   *414*
She shouldn't be.
Everyone else is sleeping soundly,
  except you and me.
They don't know about the world, obviously.
They are passing by on the other side.
Often the best place to be, Lord.
One eye on you.
One on your world.
Both eyes on the world, Lord,
  in you, through you, only.

Death is not a worry to me, Lord,   *415*
  though I am afraid of darkness,
  afraid of dying.
Afraid of my own condemnation,
  asking why I had not done better.
But you are greater than my heart, Lord.
You ask me, why I did not do worse,
  you are pleased by my triumphs,
  you see light in the darkest places of my life.
In my greatest failures
  you observe tiny fragments of virtue,
  no one else had noticed.
You gather them up at the last day.
You say to me, 'Morning at last.'

416   I've done it, Lord,
       got to bed-time.
    The world ends tonight,
       and even if it doesn't,
       mine will, in one way or another.
    Sometimes the evening comes early,
       and in the darkness I am conscious
       of nothing at all.
    But you are conscious of me, Lord.
    You've always been my great believer.
    I hear your voice saying, over and over again,
       'It doesn't matter whether you believe in me, child.
       That depends on your make-up.
       I believe in you.'

417   Those who pray badly also sleep well,
       or deserve to.
    Those who cannot pray at all are also your servants,
       doing as well as they can,
       with the faith they have,
       the doubt they possess.
    That also, no doubt, is your gift to them.
    And so I lay my head on your pillow,
       unworried by my own lack of prayer or feeling.
    You make up for it, Lord.
    You have enough faith for both of us.

418   Help me to hear the music of your life, Lord.
    It is better to be born in ignominy,
       than to leave others outside in the stable.
    Better to die in desolation
       without any comfort from man or religion,
       than to leave others similarly disadvantaged.

Better to rise again in our hearts,
   though your own life is broken and complete.
Better to come to life in others,
   that they and we may be blessed at the last.

I lie down to sleep and take my rest.   *419*
But my mind doesn't rest.
Someone has left the ignition on;
   it keeps racing round the garden.
Put your hand on the ignition, Lord.
Slow the engine down quietly
   if you cannot switch it off.
Here I am, counting sheep now.
They are jumping about in my head.
Can't you slow them down, Lord?
You should be able to.
You are their shepherd also.

Thank you Lord, for the places I did not go to,   *420*
   the friends I did not meet,
   the work I did not accept.
You went there but so did I,
   in my thought, your prayer in me.
Nothing, Lord, is ever wasted.
Nothing is lost.

421 Those who walk in darkness are part of a valued family. Which begins with a star shining brightly so that wise men can travel safely, though the star itself has no sense of its own light.

Jesus himself died in darkness, an outcast in his own society and religious tradition, and is still the great outsider. His lonely death on the cross, with its moment of utter dereliction, is seen as our point of atonement; when human nature is reduced to its utter aloneness in the solitude of each human life, which I hope may lead to the realisation that we are all uniquely loved.

422 The night comes, Lord,
    when no one can work.
Nor should we need to,
    when the day is over,
    and we return ourselves to you,
    our work to you,
    the world to you,
    ourselves to your love and keeping.
Help us to rest in your word, Lord.
Keep our minds safe from all worries,
    especially those that will not go away.
Help us to sleep until morning.

423 Ponder my words, Lord.
Listen to them closely.
As we listen to yours.
We who are too shy to speak,
    uncertain how to praise you.
Yet we do praise you.
Your love requests it.
We praise you as the sun goes down.

It is strange, Lord,   *424*
   the effect of a candle:
   so trivial a thing,
   so small a piece of wax.
And yet I light it,
   and for a little space
   the darkness is driven back,
   so that the world itself is lighter
   because of my candle,
   because of one good deed,
   because of one life.

A prayer for one who has taken his or her own life

Lord, your servant, was one of those on the ledge,   *425*
   and the ledge got narrower over the years.
It had never been very wide
   but s/he had managed to live there,
   managed to survive,
   managed to smile.

We thought (N) was doing rather well,
   things would somehow improve.
But the ledge got smaller
   until s/he had nowhere to stand.
And when s/he could no longer
   cling onto your love,
   s/he fell into your arms.

Praying the Ministry

The prayers in this section were written for use by priests, that term being used freely and including ministers of the Church generally. Many of them, however, could readily be used with little or no adaptation by other people with pastoral responsibilities, and they could also, again with a little modification, be used by people in general to pray *for* the ministry of the Church in all its forms, lay and ordained.

Sometimes the prayers may need slight adaptation to suit the user's own particular tradition. In some cases, for example, 'prayer book' may helpfully be changed to 'Bible'.

A Prayer for my Congregation

Dear Lord, bless my congregation.   426
They are your ears and your eyes in the world.
They are your arms and your legs,
    going about doing good.
Their mouth is your mouth:
    the only lips you have in this place,
    to speak your word every day of the week.

And yes, Lord,
    some of them are older than me, some younger.
But such as they are, you are,
    and I kneel before you in them.

A prayer to my congregation

427   Please use me as a priest and minister.
       Tell me how I can help you.
       Let our talk be appropriate and seemly.
       Do not burden me with talk on church architecture,
           or church finances.
       More vocations have been smothered by trivia
           than have been lost by deliberate negligence.
       Build me up.
       Stress my good points – no doubt I have some.
       Encourage me in my virtues,
           rather than rebuke me for my vices.
       My sin, like yours,
           needs to be crowded out by virtue,
           not driven out by protestation.
       Please help me,
           please love me,
           and yes . . . please respect me.
       But do not put me on a pedestal;
           it hurts so much when I fall off.

The priest in the morning

428   The priest gets up when he is able; if he is able. He
       is still a priest in pyjamas. The priest does what he
       can, but no more. He does not try to be busier
       than everyone else. He remembers that Jesus of
       Nazareth appeared to his disciples when they were
       off duty, mending their nets.
           He does not hurry himself or boss himself about.
       He knows he is not the first Christian or priest in
       the parish, and hopes he will not be the last. The
       faith he is given does not come from those who

were Christians in this place before him. His faith comes to him humbly and quietly, as he goes to the bathroom.

The priest tries to think of the things he is doing one   *429*
by one. That is the only way to stop worrying over what he cannot do. For every visit the priest makes, there are ninety-nine he does not make. For every letter he writes, there are ninety-nine he does not. The priest concentrates all his energies on the one.

Jesus said we would do greater works than he did,   *430*
not more. The priest's task is not to be busier than everyone else. It is to be more enabling. The priest does not invade other people's lives. He helps them to be priests also. He helps people to do more works and preach greater sermons than he himself ever can. So is the Lord's work carried on, and the Father glorified.

The priest takes   *431*
   one day at a time,
  as he takes
   one tablet at a time.
He dissolves it slowly
   in twelve hours of water;
   he does not gulp it all down
   in one go.
He savours it,
   sips it,
   lets it go down
   into his life
   in God's good,
   slow time.
The priest does not hurry.

432   You told us, Lord,
      that we would do
      greater things than you,
      not more.
   Help me to enable others,
      not restrict them,
      to assist their lives,
      not invade them.
   Help me to enable others
      to be your priests also.
   Then they will do greater works
      than I have done;
      and so your work will be carried on,
      our Father glorified.

433   Lord, I have a lot of duties today.
   I am borne down not by the things I do
      but by the visits I cannot make,
      the people I cannot reach
      except in the deep well
      of your prayer for them,
      and even there I fail daily.
   Help me to do what I can today with love.
   Help me to hear your voice
      in those who really need me,
      and need your love in me.
   Help me not to be deluged in trivia,
      but keep to the point – your point.
   Help me to attend and assist,
      so far as I may,
      your coming.

The priest at prayer

The priest says his prayers in church if he can. If   *434*
people keep asking him how old the church is, or
how new the prayer book, this can be difficult. In
that case a familiar place in his home may be easier.

He offers the psalm and prayer for the day with
many others. He knows he is one of a great multitude. He is not alone.

Even when he is in a hurry the priest has time to
call out to this unseen body of companions his
favourite word: Amen.

So be it. May God's kingdom come in me.

The priest's first duty   *435*
    is not to be
    surrounded by people.
It is to be alone,
    surrounded only by that love
    which created the world,
    standing on that one spot
    from which all souls are blessed.

The priest and his prayer book   *436*
    are not easily parted.
The prayer book says to the priest,
    'Open me.'
As he opens the gospels
    the priest steps into another world
    – long ago, in Galilee,

with the lame man walking,
and the blind man
beginning to see again,
the dead situations raised up.
But these things happen today
by God's grace.
And the Lord of Galilee
is the Lord of the priest's parish also.
The priest remembers this
when he closes his prayer book.
He has a closed prayer book
but an open heart.

437   It's only me, Lord,
the same as yesterday;
not much better,
a little bit older,
but, such as I am,
you use me.
Such as you are,
you bless us all.

The priest in the study

438   The more letters the priest writes, the more letters he will have to write. The more times he answers the phone and takes trouble, the more trouble there will be to take in the future. But the priest who never answers letters will, in the end, have none to answer. The priest who never visits will, in the end, have no one to visit.

The priest then does what every Christian can. He answers each letter with love, if not always at length. He prays what every Christian prays:

'Lord – as I am able – according to your grace.'

The priest's letters need not be long, but they should   *439*
contain, if possible, a note of encouragement and
love.

The phone can also be used for this; but in a letter
kind thoughts are made 'visible', as in the bread
and wine on Sunday. Letters can be looked at again
and again.

It is a letter which we receive from Saint Paul
every Sunday, not a phone call.

The priest answers personal letters personally. He   *440*
knows he can never write to everyone, but that a
letter of goodwill or appreciation is always of value
and can be read and looked at again and again.

The priest tries to say thank you, thank you for
being alive.

Dear Lord, the phone is ringing   *441*
   and I do not know
   who is at the other end.
I do not know
   what troubles them.
I do not know
   if they need me
   or your love through me,
   or phone only for what may seem
   (though never to you)
   a trivial reason.
All this goes through my mind
   as I reach out to answer.
And no,
   I do not need to answer the phone now.
It may be better,

if I am unable to do so properly,
that I do not do so at all.
But whether I do or not,
  help me to realise it is you calling.
Help me to know this
  of the unseen caller
  – he or she is your friend.

442   The phone can be as pastoral as any visit, but it is an entrance into someone's house without warning. Please pray for the person you are about to interrupt. Ask if it is convenient to speak now, or whether you should phone back later. Always say, 'Thank you for your time.'

When you phone someone, you are knocking at their front door. There is no reason why they should open it; and if you only reach them on your seventh attempt, do not say, 'Where were you on the other six?'

443   There is nothing in the Ten Commandments which says you have to answer the phone. The phone's ringing only tells you someone is dialling your number, not that they need you – or God in you.

You are allowed to unplug the phone, just as you are allowed to take the dog for a walk.

The priest does not answer the phone unless he has time to do so properly and with love.

If he answers the phone and does not have the time, he says, 'How good of you to phone – may I ring back later?'

The priest at home

I am your servant, Lord.   444
Day by day I serve you at the altar of my life;
    kitchen sink, children off to school,
    grubby hands, friends to be collected,
    this letter written.
In all my life, Lord,
    distractions as well as matins,
    invitations as well as evensong,
    please remember I am your friend.

Forgive me, Lord,   445
    when my face gives out the wrong signals;
    when my door mat says welcome,
    but my manner doesn't;
    when I am tired or irritated,
    and my concern at something else
    comes over as neglect of others.
Help me to think of you, Lord.
Help me to rest.

If I cannot be holier than anyone else,   446
    no doubt I can be busier.
If I cannot be kinder than anyone else,
    no doubt, by my frenzied activity
    and full diary,
    I can make people beholden to me
    for one hour of that valuable time
    you have bestowed so kindly upon us all.
Lord, help me not to be a busybody,

only a body busy
with the gentle caring for your people;
only a body busy
in the slow unhurried care of that vineyard
where your virtues grow silently
in your good time.

447   Dear Lord, my child is ill.
He is in bed upstairs.
I am in my study,
   waiting for him to wake.
Help me to remember, Lord,
   as the phone goes,
   that he is my parishioner also.
In caring for him,
   I care for you.
In waiting for him to wake,
   I wait for you.

448   If two people want to see me at the same time, I am lucky to be so popular. Perhaps I can introduce them to each other, as Jesus introduced Peter to Andrew, though they had been brothers all their lives, as had James and John.

The priest does not try to be busier than anyone else. If he does, he will leave a hole in people's lives when he dies. He seeks to help people to live their own lives more fully. The only void he leaves in people's lives is filled . . . by love.

Of course, the phone call, 449
   the knock on the door
   needn't be an interruption, Lord,
   an intrusion into my privacy
   just as I was going out.
It could, after all, be you in your weakness
   at the other end of the line,
   on the other side of the door.
And I may find what started
   as a nuisance to my day
   becoming, by your grace,
   a help to its continuing.

Make my home, Lord, your home; 450
   your dwelling place on earth.
Help me to be like Martha
   and make people tea.
Help me to be like Mary
   and listen.

My wife made tea for you today, Lord. 451
I wonder if you noticed –
   that young couple who came
   to put in their banns;
   that old woman troubled
   over her son's going into hospital.
And no, Lord, I do not suppose
   she has fed the five thousand all at once,
   but little by little over the years
   a great multitude has been nourished
   by her love.
Help me to remember
   she is your celebrant also;
   the coffee and biscuits sacraments of your love,
   of your presence in the world.

452   Help me to do one thing at a time, Lord.
Help me not to rush;
    to be occupied totally
    in this present moment,
    this present situation and person.
It is your child I speak to, Lord,
    your brother or sister
    in the chair beside me,
    in the world, living at the same time.
Lord, help me to see you in distractions also.
Help me, though I do not feel like it, to smile.

453   I have all the time in the world.
You gave it to me.
I am not hurried at all, Lord;
    quite rested,
    waiting for you to come
    in this person
    and this call on the time
    you have showered upon me.
Oh no . . . it's that phone again.
I can hear it calling me,
    threatening me, pulling me.
I'm coming, Lord.
Help me to say, 'Amen.'

The priest in the parish

The priest is remembered for *how* he visits, not for 454
how much. A little visit in the Lord's name is worth
great riches.

The first visit the priest makes to his parish is by
living in it, and praying for the people, loving them
day by day. All other visits, on the phone or by letter, are an extension of this first visit.

It matters more how a priest visits than how many
times he knocks on someone's door. The priest
always has time for people. He is never in a hurry
to be away from anybody, though he may sometimes
be in a hurry to somebody.

Dear Lord, 455
   I can never do everything.
Help me therefore
   to do what I can with love.
Help me to offer you
   my five loaves
   and two small fish.
They do not seem much
   with a world to be fed,
   a nation to be visited.
But, as well as I can,
   I do what I can,
   going about my few visits
   and one or two solitary letters.
You will take them,
   you will use them.
Help me to do your work, Lord,
   but not your job.

211

456   A visit is still a visit, even when people are not at home. Leave a kind note, not rushed. Do not let people feel you consider your journey wasted. Always visit as if you were on earth for this person only, but never presume on being asked. Be as grateful for time on people's doorsteps as you are for time in their kitchens. Their doorstep also, and garden, are part of their home. Visit as if theirs was the only home or situation you cared about in your whole life. Talk about what concerns and interests them. Find your love and reward there. Your main contribution to any conversation lies in listening.

457   No one can be everywhere. By being born in Bethlehem, Jesus could not be born in Cana of Galilee; at least, not in the same way.

Being a Christian is a particular business, as well as a universal one. We can only do what we can, according to the limitations and opportunities of our own temperament.

By living in one parish, the priest does not live in any other. By living in one parish, the priest helps to bless the whole world.

458   Help me to say, 'How are you?', Lord.
Help me to ask after other people
    with love but not intrusion.
Help me not to rush into the sanctuary
    of people's lives.
Help me, if I am there,
    to walk quietly,
    to remove my sandals.
Help me to know, as Moses did,
    the place whereon I stand is holy.

Lord, help me to visit others   *459*
    in your name, in your way,
    with your humility,
    as you yourself visit me.
I am your servant, Lord,
    before I am anybody else's.
Help me to remember my duty,
    not to be popular,
    not to feed all the five thousand myself,
    but only those closest to me,
    those whom the world has forgotten.
Help me to gather up the forgotten people,
    the forgotten parts of all our lives.
Help me to touch those parts
    that others cannot touch,
    and help me to receive their blessing

The priest as sinner

The priest's job is not to hear other people's confes-   *460*
sions of failure, but only to live with his own. Because
he is conscious always of this failure, others may be
led to stand beside him, kneel beside him, and say,
'The state of the world is my fault. I am to blame.'

Help me when I feel down, Lord,   *461*
    when I feel the world is against me,
    when the world *is* against me;
    when I feel alone with no one to help,
    and even you, especially you, seem far away.
It is when I am weak, Lord,
    that you are strong.
It is when I fail and am cast down
    that you come to life in others.

213

462   The priest gives glory to God in his weakness. He
       knows it is in his weakness that others can be
       blessed. He does not preach to people from an
       upstairs window. In the darkness and difficulties
       of their own lives, the priest is their friend.

463   Every life is a history of mistakes.
       It depends only on what we do with them.
       Help me to use mine wisely, Lord.
       I may not get another chance
           to fail in this way again.
       Help me to use my failures as stones
           fitted together, one on top of another,
           to make a building where others can come;
           a life where others feel welcome,
           unthreatened, because they are sinners too.
       When I am weak, Lord,
           in all these failures I carry round,
           then you are strong.

464   The priest is a sinner.
       Above all, he knows what it is to try and fail.
       He says,
           'May God forgive us all.
           May God forgive me especially
           day by day.'
       He asks it every Sunday.
       It is the first day
           of the rest of his life;
           the day when all his congregation
           seek to begin again.

To be a priest is to be a Christian in a particular way. 465
The priest represents the Church, as all Christians
do. He represents Christ on earth, as each Christian
does.

The priest blesses the bread and wine, on behalf
of all Christians. The priest asks, 'May God forgive
us all, myself included,' day by day.

Help me to live 466
   with my sins, Lord.
They are my companions daily,
   keeping me low,
   enabling me to remember
   I am a sinner on the earth's face,
   as are all your people.
Linked to them
   by these failures,
   these limitations,
   day by day in your grace
   we go forward together.

The priest in church

To some extent the priest's life is a public life. He 467
wears clothes he does not feel like wearing. He wears
expressions he may not feel underneath: joy at a chris-
tening when he himself has great sorrow; sorrow at a
bereavement when he himself may not feel personal
loss. In all of this the priest tries to show care and feeling for people in their different stations of life.

He tries, by his love and attention to the smallest
detail, to make other people's lives and deaths his
own experience. He tries to say, 'May God be present
in your living and in your departing.'

215

468   Those inside the congregation ask for signs, Lord;
           big services, grand occasions,
           alleluias in your market place.
       Those outside need wisdom to convert them;
           but we can only offer our lives, Lord,
           broken, and in union with your own.

469   Help me to remember, Lord,
           at this baptism,
           that I only pour the water.
       Another baptises
           while I only stand
           at the door of the church and say,
           'How nice to see you again,' and,
           'I hope you have a safe journey home.'
       As I baptise with water
           like your servant John,
           another comes to touch the people's hearts.
       As I give out service sheets,
           smile at the little girl who's chewing hers
           and pause to ask her name . . .
           in all of this your Spirit comes
           in your way, not mine.
       There stands among us
           in this congregation
           one whom I know not; but you do.
       Even so, Lord Jesus,
           come quickly.

Lord, I have another funeral. 470
And yet it is not just another funeral
   but their 'only' one.
This life now ended
   had its own beginning long ago;
   parents I never knew,
   visitors to greet this birth
   who have gone before.
And now I am left
   at the end of this life
   to make sense of it;
   to commend it back to you.
Help me to listen
   to the lives of those I have not known.
Help me to hear
   the sound of their childhood,
   their career,
   their families, their successes . . .
Help me in all of this
   to hear the sound
   of your life in them.
Then, as the hearse comes,
   and the men in black carry your child in,
   I will not think, 'Another funeral
   to be got through in twenty minutes,'
   but your love
   in one unique life
   to be recalled
   and set forth with praise.

It is Christmas, Lord; 471
   our usual carol service.
And I get to read the last gospel;
   as usual, I have the last word.
Help me to remember, Lord,

now that the teacher has read,
and the publican and the local policeman,
that I who read last
do not represent this community at all.
I represent only you,
    who are outside society.
Help me to remember,
    when the church is full,
    those who are not here
    because your kindness,
    through our ministry,
    has not yet called them.
Help me to speak to the empty pew also,
    to those who are awaiting
    your invitation to come.

472   People expect sermons of me, Lord,
        prayers to be taught,
        sacraments to be remembered,
        rites of passage to be performed;
        and yes, Lord, I try to provide these
        as your servant John the Baptist did.
    Remember him?
    He was your cousin;
        gave new life to your people.
    But giving sacraments is never enough.
    Learning prayers, teaching customs,
        all of this falls short;
        unless, like you,
        we give our life gently day by day,
        poured out . . . no hurry here at all . . .
        gently,
        constantly,
        always for others.

Lord, I have a baptism,   473
     another baptism;
     though it is not so to them.
For this family,
     this is their only child;
     for this child,
     it is their only entrance
     into your Church.
Help me to welcome them, Lord,
     as Simeon blessed and welcomed you.
Help me to know
     the world will never be the same again
     because of this christening,
     this child.
I have a part to play
     in their future,
     even if, like Simeon,
     I do not see them again,
     only pray for them.

The priest on Sunday

God does not mind the priest hurrying his prayers   474
to him. The congregation does. A brief 'Lord help
me' is most pleasing to God. The shortest 'alleluia'
is welcome. But the priest only sees his congregation once a week. He does not carry them about in
his heart in quite the same way. He cannot talk to
them all the time as he can to God.

He leaves time, therefore, before the service, for
himself; after the service, for them. He asks after
people, wishing them well. If someone is away, he
asks after them or sends a message The priest cannot do everything himself, but can set in motion
kind thoughts and enquiries that reach out. The
worship itself reaches up.

475   The priest recalls the life of Jesus every Sunday at the Lord's table. He shows forth the life of an obscure carpenter who loved his friends and enemies till the end. He proclaims this way of love, and tells it, even if he cannot live it well himself. The priest spends one day showing forth the life of Jesus in the bread and wine. The other six days he tries to live it.

476   The priest greets people as they come into church, by smiling at them when he says, 'The Lord be with you'. He says goodbye to them at the end, one by one, in his heart. He knows his people by name. He loves and values them.

        He welcomes them into the world at their baptism. He sees them out of the world at their funeral. He says, 'May the Lord bless your coming in and your going out, from this time forth and for evermore', and he does his best for them in between.

477   The priest greets everyone on Sunday even if he does not know or remember them, for other people change and get older, not only the priest.

        The priest wishes people goodbye one by one. When he asks the blessing, he says, 'The Lord be with you', and knows the Lord is in every soul he meets. The priest says 'Amen' to every life. So be it.

        May God's kingdom come in you.

A priest's first duty is to smile.   478
Of course, we do not necessarily
   smile with our lips.
With our eyes, ears, hands or feet
   we try to say, 'I love you.
     Come to me all who travail
     and are heavy laden
     and I will refresh you.'
Dear Lord. help me to smile,
   but not just with my mouth.
Help me to say, 'How are you?'
More important,
   help me to wait for an answer;
   and to wait and listen till it is given,
   in your way and your time.

The priest as preacher

The priest is a pastor or shepherd. The only true   479
weapon he has is his voice. He calls people to him
by the way he lives, and by the way he reads or
commends the gospel. He gives value to all those
he meets.

Those who hear the priest's voice come to him
Then they may pass him by, on their way to the
master. The priest rejoices when people forget his
name, or do not know he is there The priest, however, also needs to be loved.

480   The priest prepares his sermon as well as he can. It is more important to prepare the preacher than to prepare the sermon. Even so, the priest reads the gospel every week at Communion

He seeks to tell the good news that we are all loved and forgiven, and have our own part to play in the redemption of God's world. The priest wishes only to love and speak to the people as Jesus of Nazareth would, if he were alive today. Which of course he is, in their hearts.

481   What a priest is speaks louder than what he says. How a priest lives matters more than where.

He is always a servant, even when he exhorts himself to lead, or to commend: always a servant, never a master.

482   It is my first sermon, Lord.
The people are waiting
    to see if I can manage it,
    to see if I can manage anything.
Help me to speak your words, Lord.
One of your words in kindness
    is better than a thousand condemnations.
Help me to know the value of any sermon
    does not depend on my preparation alone.
My uncertainty as how to speak
    you will use anyway;
      but the result lies with you who give the words
      and those who hear them.
As soon as I have spoken,
    they become your words, Lord.
Help me to bless my people
    as they take the words away.

To some extent the priest is the sermon. What the   483
priest is matters more than what he says. The priest
speaks best with his mouth shut.

   The messenger matters more than the message?
Not quite. But . . . the messenger is part of the message. He or she must love the people.

I will not offer my people, Lord,   484
   that which costs me nothing.
Help me to remember daily,
   my people are your people first of all.
My friends are your friends
   seeing things in your gospel
   that I miss;
   having opportunities
   I am not given.
Help me then to advance on my knees
   as I serve them, as I pray for them.
As I climb the north face of your pulpit
   Sunday by Sunday,
   help me to see the promised land,
   your promise, in your people
   first of all.

When I am weak, you are strong, and when I seem   485
to be strong bless me and forgive me then especially.

486   Lord, help me not to feel sea-sick
            as I get into your boat and,
            looking over the side,
            notice the deep waters below;
            so many fish, so many possibilities,
            and I myself am conscious
            of none of them;
            only of Andrew's oars
            and Peter's tackle,
            James' sandals
            and all the fishing nets
            waiting to be used.
     The crowd are still there,
            pressing down to the water's edge,
            and though I may see
            only one or two of them,
            by your grace
            I speak through them
            to a great number.

487   Lord, help me to preach.
     Help me to tell your story
            to your people.
     Help me to listen first;
            to hear the sound of Galilee's waves
            and the seagulls calling
            and the boats being pulled up
            over unwilling shingle onto the beach.
     Help me to listen to your voice,
            and as I hear the sound
            of your life and death
            to tell it,
            and so share in many resurrections.

I do not confess my sins, Lord,   *488*
   I confess my virtues:
   those services I conducted 'well',
   those times (there have been some of them)
   when the words you gave me
   went straight out to your people
   without blockage, without interruption.
The congregation hung onto my lips
   because I hung onto your word
   and did not let it go among the week's trivia.
I saw you there, and stayed with you.
I confess to you, Lord, all my virtues,
   all my satisfactions.
Bless them, receive them,
   use them for your mercy.
My sins, Lord, I have no need to confess.
I am ashamed of them.
They bring me low.
But when I am low
   I am close to you anyway,
   and tied to my people
   by a thousand shortcomings.

The priest at meetings

'The Lord is king, be the wardens never so impatient.   *489*
The Lord reigns, be the committees never so unquiet.'

   Meetings are not perhaps the best medium for the coming of the kingdom. People are meeting to discuss finance, buildings, time of services . . .

   There are differences of views here. Before every meeting the priest prays, 'Lord, as you will. Lord, in your time, in your way.'

490   To administer church affairs, or any affairs, is to minister or serve in a particular way. The priest does not always, or perhaps ever, have this gift.

He prays therefore before each meeting, 'Lord, as you will', and 'Lord, in your way'.

The priest helps all administrators to feel their administration is part of the ministry of Christ.

The priest is a servant; he does not try to boss other people about. He does not try to boss himself about. He tries to wait on God's love and help others to do the same.

The woman priest

491   I am a woman, Lord,
      as your mother was,
      and your sisters,
      if you had them.
Since Mary of Magdala
      you have had many sisters.
And now you have another, in me.
Help me to remember, Lord,
      the priest's heart
      is always maternal.
The priest always has
      more children in the faith
      than can be realised.
Like other Christians
      we never know
      those that have been brought to faith
      through our words.

Dear Lord, I am a woman,   492
   and for some people
   that ministry may be an offence.
They are used to men
   reading your gospel,
   telling your story,
   as you were a man in Galilee
   calling your disciples after you.
And yet, Lord,
   your heart was maternal.
You called us your children,
   longed to gather under your wings
   the small sparrows of society,
   discarded and left out.
Help me, Lord, to gather under your wings
   those you have given me,
   and those who may find me a problem.
Help my heart at least
   to be loving towards them,
   you who love us
   as a father and a mother
   love their children.

Lord, I am a woman priest   493
   preparing for my first eucharist.
Help me to remember,
   as I prepare the bread and wine,
   how your own supper was prepared long ago
   by one man carrying a pitcher of water on his head.
If he was humble enough
   to do work previously reserved for women,
   may I be humble enough
   to do work previously reserved for men.
I follow this figure, Lord,

into your sanctuary today.
He goes before me.
He has had long practice,
   as you have,
   in learning the essence of our calling:
   to serve others,
   to do the works
   others are too proud to do;
   this service only
   will lead us to the feast.

The priest at rest

494   Like everyone else, the priest needs rest; space to be himself, and hear life calling to him in its own particular way. None of us can catch all the nuances of that love which the Father has in store for each of us. We can only catch those nuances for which temperament or experience has at present prepared us.

    The priest needs rest. Like Jesus of Nazareth, he needs to go sometimes to the other side of the Sea of Galilee.

495   Lord, help me not
   to do too much.
Help me not to exceed
   that activity limit
   you yourself set
   on any life
   including your own.

Only so many things can be done,
   not more.
Only so many letters written,
   visits made.
The activity, Lord,
   is limited.
Your love for us
   is without end.

Help me to stand back a little, Lord;   *496*
   to get in Peter and Andrew's boat,
   if they are still around,
   and go to the other side
   of whatever Galilee
   you yourself have provided.
Help me to rest,
   not to feel I have to read all the paper;
   I am allowed to 'skip',
   dwell on those few passages I read,
   become 'myself', and not compete
   with those who visit more,
   preach longer,
   are 'more successful'.
Help me to do your work, Lord,
   and leave others, mainly yourself,
   to do your job.

The priest's aim is to be made redundant. He works   *497*
for the day when all God's people will be, not clergy
dressed up, but priests clothed with God's Spirit in
their own lives.

   He knows there is no shortage of clergy, only of
Christians. There is no shortage of 'Christians', only
of the Holy Spirit.

498   Lord, help me to be faithful,
        but not to push the point too far,
        or my faithfulness further than I can bear;
        as Peter did
        when he got out of his fishing boat
        and followed you alone across the waves.
    We can't do everything, Lord.
    We need the security of the boat
        and our companions there.
    The journey of the boat itself,
        like your presence with us,
        is without end.

The priest in the evening

499   Lord, I am getting older,
        and it occurs to me,
        one day the pulpit steps
        will be too steep,
        the stairway to your altar
        too difficult for my aching limbs.
    Help me to remember then,
        as the hands on my clock
        move round the face,
        that they only bring me
        nearer to you.

I will not be asked,   *500*
   at the end of my life,
   how many sermons I have visited
   upon my people,
   only how many visits
   I have turned into sermons
   by my care,
   and your love through me.

Lord, what is a priest?   *501*
I tell your story,
   but often do not hear it myself.
I visit your people,
   but often have no sense
   of you visiting me.
I break the bread
   and bless the wine for others,
   but who will bless it for me?
Who will give me your cup to drink?
And then, Lord,
   as I get older
   the prayers I have offered
   do not seem any deeper.
They fade away
   and my sense of things dwindles.
Yet in all this you stay beside me
   and comfort me.
In old age and failure also
   you are my friend.

502   Dear Lord, I am ill.
       I cannot do the things I used to.
       My life fractures.
       The years have taken their toll.
       So many weddings,
          with the brides not looking back
          to say thank you.
       So many baptisms
          of those I do not see again.
       So many funerals
          of people I have not met in this life,
          or ever known.
       As my health crumbles
          and my mind collapses,
          help others to know,
          even if I cannot,
          that the Lord is King,
          and comes to his world
          in his own time
          and his own way.
       I am limited to the sacraments
          and the frailties of this human condition,
          but when I collapse,
          the seeds planted
          will still grow.

503   Lord, I am still your priest,
          as my robes of office are taken away
          and I am no longer indispensable
          to a wide circle of your friends.
       Help me to remember
          I am always your servant,
          still your minister,
          always indispensable to you.

I am reaching my end, Lord; 504
   my end, not yours;
   my end, not other people's.
Others are in the pulpit now,
   opening my prayer book,
   turning over the pages,
   finding insights I never thought of.
As I leave, Lord, may you begin.
Carry on your work
   with candles I have helped to light,
   or not always been able to.
My end, Lord, is not my people's end;
   nor mine either,
   as all things begin again with you.

Lord, I am busier than you are. 505
I have already lived on earth
   longer than you did,
   made more visits, fed more people,
   preached more sermons
   than you ever managed.
Help me, Lord,
   in the time I have left,
   not to lengthen my years
   but deepen my love.
May your life continue in me.
And may my declining years
   be your opportunity,
   your continuing.

506   Lord, help me to take it easy.
One day, after all,
    I will have to hand all this back to you.
And no, I am not indispensable
    (although I am to you),
    and my memory is going
    (have I told you this before?).
But as my memory gets shorter
    and my sermons longer,
    help me to remember only this:
    you do not forget me.

The priest as bishop

507   The light that shone on God's first bishops at Bethlehem illuminated their lives and drew them to our attention. It did not create them.

    The spotlight of the world or the media's interest can fall on lots of other things. But loving your sheep and knowing them by name remain to a Christian, the most news-worthy.

508   How do you choose bishops, Lord?
This light that so startled them,
    this spotlight on them,
    did not in itself consecrate them.
Only made visible
    to our own poor vision
    what they had been doing all their lives.
Counting their sheep daily,
    gathering them in every night,

tending them,
blessing them.
While Caesar and his government proclaim,
'Count everybody',
your first bishops said, and still say,
'Everybody counts'.

This hat is heavy, Lord,   *509*
yet I do not wear it for myself.
These tongues of fire
reach out to bless and enable
all your children.
Each of them has his or her proper part,
gift of that one Spirit
which unites us all.
I rejoice in my own gift, Lord,
which is the recognition
of your Spirit in others.

For those of us who have been called   *510*
to serve as priests, Lord,
there can be no promotion.
From then on it is downhill
all the way.
I came in from those hills
long ago at Bethlehem.
Your light did not consecrate me;
that had happened long before.
Over so many nights,
many days,
these little rescues of your people,

235

these constant kindnesses and feedings,
   which your love laid on me.
I am still a priest, Lord,
   as the mitre descends.
Still a deacon,
   always a deacon,
   as I grip your staff.
I need it for walking, Lord.
   I cannot manage without it.
On windy days,
   in uncertain conditions,
   it always reminds me:
   you rescue me,
   and watch over me,
   daily.

511   I look down at your crib, Lord,
   I who am made your bishop,
   and come in from the cold.
I look at this poor child,
   I do not know his name,
   only that you love him
   while his mother prays
   and Joseph holds the lantern
   so I can see him clearly.
This child I confirm,
   this child I ordain to your service.
What will become of him or her,
   to what far lands will
   he or she travel?
I do not know, Lord,
   only that you will love them,
   and I who visit them
   in the morning of their lives,
   pray for them daily.

A prayer for those who drift away

And did their love last, Lord? 512
And if it failed to,
   was it any less valid for that?
Those who had heard you
   and followed you
   and been overtaken by other courses,
   help them at the end, Lord,
   to remember you.

Epilogue

Dear Lord, send us priests. 513
Don't let the door-to-door
   delivery of your love
   be a thing of the past.
Don't let the delivery of your word
   Sunday by Sunday
   be a thing only our grandparents remember.
Lord, send us priests today.

Index